BRiGHTON:
THE SiXTiES

Christopher Horlock

S.B. Publications

DEDICATION

This, my sixth book on Brighton, is dedicated (like my first) to my amazing wife (Roz) and children (Charlotte, aged 14 and George, aged 10). Six Brighton books in six years is a lot for a family to take particularly with me rushing around here, there and everywhere, gathering all the material needed, 'phoning people, hours at reference libraries viewing microfilm newspapers, then months of work on the PC typing it all up; really and truly, I should have been with them, enjoying their company.

By the same author -
Brighton, The Century In Photographs I
Brighton, The Century In Photographs II
Brighton and Hove Then And Now I
Brighton and Hove Then And Now II
The Neat And Nippy Guide To Brighton's History

First published in 2006 by S. B. Publications
Tel: 01323 893498   Email: sbpublications@tiscali.co.uk

ISBN 1-85770-304-9

Designed and Typeset by EH Graphics (01273) 515527

CONTENTS

ACKNOWLEDGEMENTS

It's a *long* story, but most of the photographs in this book were actually saved from a skip situated in Robert Street, Brighton, when the newspaper group Southern Publishing (long before their move to Hollingbury in more recent years) had a clear out and threw most of their 1960s photos away for some reason. Probably a new managerial broom sweeping clean. Many were rescued by staff photographer John Barrow and taken back to his home in Chelston Avenue, Hove, where he 'sat on them' (not literally) for a number of years, before giving the whole lot to me.

Dozens have helped directly or indirectly with the compilation of this book. I can't thank the many, many people I talked to about their memories of the decade individually, but special mention must be made of (in no particular order) the late Steve Benz, Jacqueline Pollard, Douglas d'Enno, John Royce, Trevor Povey, David Courtney and ex-policeman of the time, David Rowland, who were particularly forthcoming.

I have to thank Simon Bradshaw, former editor of the Argus, for permission to use all the old photographs and quotations from past newspapers. Dr Anthony Seldon, former Headmaster of Brighton College, let me quote from his book *Brave New City*, and the college archivist, Joyce Heater, cheerfully tracked down a picture of the Queen's visit in 1962, Jeff Wareing, of the Isetta Owners Club, allowed me to use a picture of his 'bubble car', still going strong forty years after it was made! Thanks are also extended to the staff of Hove Reference Library who let me have free reign over their microfilm machine and endless reels of film, and Brighton History Centre which did the same.

Sources and References

Newspapers were obviously the best source material for information needed to compile this book. These included back editions of the *Argus* (which used to be the *Evening Argus*), *Brighton and Hove Gazette* and *Brighton and Hove Herald*. I also used a large number of lecture notes used by James S Gray, which are always an accurate source for basic facts and figures to get me started.

The main local books consulted were *Life In Brighton,* by Clifford Musgrave (John Hallewell Publications, 1970); *Brighton Old And New,* by Antony Dale and James Gray (EP Publishing, 1976); *Brave New City,* by Anthony Seldon (Pomegranate Press, 2002); *Foul Deeds and Suspicious Deaths Around Brighton,* by Douglas d'Enno (Wharncliffe Books, 2004); *Brighton and Hove Cinemas,* by Allen Eyles (Tempus Publishing 2003) and, of course, the trusty *Encyclopaedia of Brighton,* by Tim Carder (East Sussex County Libraries, 1990). I also used *The Sixties,* by Francis Wheen (Century Publishing, in association with Channel Four TV Company, 1982) and countless Internet websites on the 1960s.

Special Notes

Amounts of money are given in old pounds, shillings and pence. Before metrication in 1971, twenty shillings made a pound and twelve pennies made a shilling, So ten shillings (written 10/-) was 120 pennies and would be 50p today, three shillings (3/-) would be 15p and so on. Two pounds and two shillings, written as £2/2/- (or £2/2/0) would be £2.10 today.

Distances, measurements etc, are given in old imperial units. I'm sure anyone desperate for the metric equivalents will be able to work them out.

Quotes are taken directly from newspapers of the period; the film reviews at the start of each year are obviously only part of what was written. Other quotes are occasionally slightly edited or condensed and if sometimes the punctuation - or lack of it - seems strange, it's usually reproduced exactly as it appeared in print.

Despite a fair bit of effort, I was unable to trace the copyright holders of several photographs, mainly portraits of personalities of the period issued in postcard form; no publisher's name or distribution firm appear on any of them and I'm hoping no major transgression has taken place by including them.

NOT QUITE SWINGIN' BRIGHTON

Apart from a chapter by Clifford Musgrave in *Life In Brighton*, no one has written about 1960s Brighton in any detail, so researching this book meant starting with his account, then wading through nearly every *Argus, Brighton and Hove Herald* and *Brighton and Hove Gazette* for the years 1960-1969. I also went through the last few years of the 1950s too, just to 'set the scene' as it were and see something of the origins of many 1960s developments, and dipped into the early 1970s, to see what came next. The Argus was, and still is, a daily paper, the Herald and Gazette were weekly, so all in all I must have trawled through several thousand papers to try to get the overview of Brighton I needed. In all, it took some three years to research just ten years of history!

I was expecting (and kind of hoping) to find 'swingin' Brighton' very much in evidence, paralleling London, with reports of outrageous 'free' behaviour, people making love not war, articles on miniskirts and PVC fashion, flower power, horror at the young's new drug-taking habits, complaints about student behaviour at Sussex University, protest marches about the Vietnam War, etc., etc.

Strangely, although these stories were there, I had to dig pretty deep to discover them. What I did find in 1960s Brighton - again and again - was a town (as it was then) rebuilding itself to an unprecedented and obsessive degree. Construction projects - both large and small - seem almost endless, all taking place in just the ten years of the decade. The bit was well and truly between the Corporation's teeth and had you stuck a pin anywhere into a map of Brighton at this time, it wouldn't have been too far from some major redevelopment. Well-known projects included the building of the first Churchill Square (a 1959 plan for this is seen opposite), the modernisation of the Lanes (with Brighton Square being built) and the now notorious Top Rank entertainment building on the corner of West Street resulting in the loss of the SS Brighton ice rink. New housing was also a priority and the decade saw high-rise flats going up in several areas, including six huge blocks astride an area between Carlton Hill and Albion Hill. These would change Brighton's topography out of all recognition; the map of certain areas would have to be completely redrawn. Edward Street would also be widened, a new police HQ built (in John Street) and the tower block to the east of the Royal Sussex County Hospital would come to dominate Eastern Road. The Bristol Estate housing development would be completed above Kemp Town, so would the Hollingdean Estate (both started in the 1950s). More high-rise flats would go up off Trafalgar Street (Theobald House), between St James's Street and Edward Street, between Upper St James's Street and Eastern Road and also at Whitehawk. And I could go on!

Much would be swept away so these buildings could be constructed. Eighteen streets were lost just for the Churchill Square development (albeit over a period of many years). The Blackman Street area would ultimately be decimated. Most of Edward Street was rendered unrecognisable, where the resultant loss of small shops on the southern side is still ongoing today.

Several fine old theatres came down (which today would have made ideal homes for Brighton Festival events and fringe theatre); the original Bedford Hotel (of the 1820s) went up in flames, to be rebuilt as a slab tower, and the West Pier would be partially closed down at the end of the decade (1970). It was a time of relentless, non-stop, almost brutal planning decisions, made with the very best of

intentions for the town, but not results.

Anthony Seldon, in his recent book, *'Brave New City'* castigates the decade as being 'the locust years' when much was stripped bare and little of substance replaced it. The chapter in his book, 'The Rape Of Brighton' says: 'Some older buildings and structures had to go, but the fact that so many buildings were destroyed in a town that could match any in the country, including Bath and Cheltenham, for the quality and elegance of its Georgian and Regency architecture, is a tragedy not just for Brighton and Hove but for the country. Future generations will demand to know the names of the barbarians, and the reasons why so many poor and ugly structures were put up in place of the beautiful or historic.'

Seldon includes a list, following the above, citing the city's 'twelve worst architectural moments'; seven buildings or groups of buildings given were either planned or built in the 1960s.

Some projects, once up and running, either ran out of steam or just didn't work. Most ludicrous was the widening of Edward Street, which was meant to be the start of a dual carriageway leading well into Kemp Town. It seems that only when it reached Freshfield Road did those responsible realise that Brighton College would actually be in the way of any further extension! The traffic bottleneck in this area is something still being lived with today. Also the plan to site a new town hall somewhere in Brighton during the decade, after years and years of wrangling and being moved here, there and everywhere, was - surprisingly - abandoned.

In short, page after page after page of 1960s local newspapers show something, somewhere in Brighton either being knocked down, rebuilt, redeveloped - or plans for these. Any empty area, awaiting redevelopment, was often turned into a temporary car park along the way. It's said that Brighton escaped the worse excesses of 1960s architecture and 'modernisation'. The Old Town area may have, but other places definitely didn't. Its two most prestigious projects - the original Churchill and Brighton Squares - are now both dismissed as 1960s kitsch, one large scale, one small, although Brighton Square at least retained the human dimensions of the ancient area it occupied. Queen's Road on its eastern side, between Church Street and the station, was rendered characterless and became a sterile hotchpotch of graph-paper buildings, as was much of North Street's northern side, where Prudential House still looms large, at present operating as hotel accommodation.

I could go on - and on - but I think the point's made. And if all the above sounds one great big muddle of plans and schemes without too much thought for how they would all relate to each other or what it would all mean in terms of environmental impact - it was exactly that.

And the local reaction to all this? As you'll see, and as you'd expect, conservation groups like the astute Regency Society saw through it all and began using very untypical language (for them) when assessing its worth. A real skewer was when their annual report of 1968 likened the new Top Rank building to a public convenience. Residents were probably too dazzled by it all to really know what was going on and how it would eventually look. Very few letters appeared in the local newspapers challenging any of it. All around them, locally and nationally, the message of the sixties was that progress was a good thing and the way forward; technology - in the form of modern buildings - was the answer to everything, and Brighton was being swamped with them.

But despite all this 'progress' and effort to 'regenerate' the place, the powers-that-be in Brighton still clearly - but strangely - had one municipal foot firmly entrenched in the 1950s. And this foothold was how the town saw itself as a tourist resort. It's very contradictory to the 'new town' image the town was taking on.

Advertising material for the early sixties shows Brighton still promoting itself 100% as a family holiday resort of B&B accommodation, Punch and Judy shows, crabbing at Black Rock and day trips to nearby, picturesque Stanmer or Rottingdean. Both the Palace Pier and West Pier were fully operative at this time. The Royal Pavilion was the key tourist attraction, closely followed by the 'historic' Lanes area (before its eventual revamp). The town's publicity brochures for these years (running to over a hundred pages then) point up these family-orientated, 'what you expect from a seaside resort', type of attractions again and again.

As background to this outlook it has to be remembered that many amenities and aspects of Brighton life we now take for granted just didn't exist then. The conference trade was very low-key in the first half of the decade. The Brighton Centre, taking large conferences and staging pop concerts wouldn't be up and running until 1977. In the early 1960s there was no 'clubbing' (dancing at nightclubs) to the extent it goes on today. The population was more fixed, areas of the town were still communities and 'high-rise' was an architectural term people were just getting their heads round.

Despite being labelled 'the swingin' sixties', the pace of life forty years ago was still fairly sedate and expectations were lower. Fewer people owned cars and most visitors came to the town by train and used buses to get around. More people than you'd think still didn't have a TV at this time and those that did had small fuzzy black and white sets with very limited programming.

The moral tone of the early 1960s Brighton was - like virtually everywhere else - extremely conservative. Small, but highly established rituals took place such as the national anthem being played before every cinema and theatre presentation and everyone standing respectfully silent while it rang out - and not moving until the last note had died away. Nationally, homosexuality and abortion were both illegal at the start of the decade and the death penalty was still in place for murder. Family planning in Brighton was only available to engaged couples, determined by evidence of an engagement ring and a date for the wedding.

We also get some idea of the town's ethical outlook when certain 1960s films were vetted to see if they were suitable for showing in the town. This job, due to County Council reorganisation, left the jurisdiction of Brighton Corporation (its so-called Watch Committee) and fell for some reason to a Fire Brigade Committee, who it was felt, 'had the necessary expertise.' In 1967, the film Ulysses – which had a certificate from the British Board of Film Censors – was banned, yet a year later, I - A Woman - which didn't - was passed.

Politically, Brighton saw an extraordinary event in October 1964, when Councillor Denis Hobden became the first Labour MP, not just in Brighton, but also in the whole of Sussex.

There's a huge amount of material I'd liked to have included in the pages which follow, but had to leave out because of space, or because certain topics, although fascinating background material to the decade, aren't exclusively Brighton; they were going on everywhere. For example, I wanted to list some of the new cars that were coming onto the roads in 1960s Brighton. The local papers gave huge coverage to new vehicles because, obviously, ownership was on the increase during the 1960s and many new models were available.

Also, trawling through the local papers revealed all manner of really interesting and quirky stories that can't be detailed also because of space. So, sadly, the reader will never know the stories I found headed by the likes of - 'Built Own Boat In First Floor Flat', 'Woman Nazi Is Living As A Man', 'William The Goat Shows Off', ' or even 'It Looks As If Wigs Have Come To Stay.' There were dozens of others.

Many established, often annual, events - such as the Speed Trials, the London to Brighton Veteran Car run, Regency Festival, Home Life exhibition, the open-air art show on the seafront near the West Pier, Brighton Scout's Gang Show and Bob-a-Job week, the student Rag Week, Brighton Music Festival, the Deep Sea Anglers' competitions, shows by local amateur groups, etc, were all taking place at this time, but most can only be mentioned in passing here.

What also comes through clearly, in 1960s Brighton, at a domestic level, is a huge sense of community in most areas, with the papers devoting masses of space to local groups and their activities - Drama companies, Church groups, WI's, Townswomen's Guilds, Boy's Brigade companies, Scout groups and any number of sports and social clubs. There was even the Sussex Magic Circle, which met at the Langford's Hotel each month. Many of these, of course, are still thriving, although a fair number have now gone.

What surfaces too is how big national issues prevalent during the 1960s are still with us today forty years later - racism, defence matters, house prices, squatting, suspicion at too many student exam passes, use of animals in medical research, whether national service should be brought back, the death penalty, quality of parenting, welfare of circus animals etc, etc. Others, but not many, like whether fluoride should go into the water supply, have been largely resolved. All these issues and many others appeared sometime or other in the local papers between 1960-1969.

Was Brighton really ruined in the 1960s, something so many people have said to me while researching this book? Was it really a case of the gains being massively disproportionate to the losses?

Whatever Brighton lost in the 1960s - and the pages that follow show that a great deal really was - what didn't get entirely swept away was its irrepressible zeal to remain buoyant, pioneering and sanguine. All the major building projects previously listed - whatever is thought now of their actual design and merit - can be seen as part of this enthusiasm to some extent and equally part of that optimistic 1960s fervour that permeated much of what was going on nationally. Technology was the way forward, and if progress meant building in a certain way, then so be it. But where Brighton's 1960s optimism and innovation uniquely came through was in several imaginative, almost visionary projects, which must be seen now to stand squarely with past Georgian and Victorian innovations. An idea like Brighton Marina, with plans finally coming to fruition during the decade, was revolutionary and probably far more daring than any other scheme of the whole 20th century. The launching of the annual Brighton Festival in 1967 was another 'first' and would grow to national significance within the artistic world in a way the early promoters never dreamed it would. Establishing Sussex University (the earliest plans for this dating back to 1911) was another landmark achievement of the 1960s; all these projects have flourished and become firmly part of today's Brighton and Hove in an enormously significant way. But it's ironic that all these - and others on a smaller scale - were not really born from Corporation initiatives or government dictates. They weren't originally generated by committees or businesses or wealthy firms with an eye only to what return they could make out of them. In 1960s Brighton, despite the huge developments described in the pages that follow, the real movers and shapers, the ones with the brilliant ideas - as in the past, when anything really spectacular happened in the town - were seemingly ordinary people (usually local) with that rarest of all municipal abilities: real vision that was positively daring, and the drive and determination to see their dream actually materialize.

Christopher Horlock *February 2006*

The Churchill Square site, 1965.

1960

Some Key Events:

January	- The foundation stone of the Aswan Dam in Egypt is laid by Nasser.
March	- Elvis Presley's only visit to the UK - his plane refuels in Scotland!
April	- The Everly Brothers visit Britain for the first time.
May	- The Beatles are turned down as Billy Fury's backing group.
June	- The BBC Television Centre opens in London.
July	- Sailor Francis Chichester sets a new cross-Atlantic record in his boat Gypsy Moth II - just forty days.
August	- Penguin Books plan to publish the complete, unexpurgated version of *Lady Chatterley's Lover* results in prosecution under obscenity laws. The Rome Olympics are held. Britain wins two gold medals.
September	- MOT for cars over ten years old introduced.
November	- John F Kennedy elected President of USA.
December	- First episode of Coronation Street is broadcast.

No 1 in the music charts at Christmas was 'I Love You' by Cliff Richard

Social Snippet - In 1960, the annual weekly wage in Britain was £14/10/8 (just over £14.50) and virtually all manual workers were only entitled to a fortnight's holiday a year.

Local Film Review: *Solomon and Sheba* (shown at the Astoria)
Without any shadow of a doubt *Solomon and Sheba* is the biggest, most stupendous and colossal production we have seen since The Ten Commandments. It is also the largest slice of hokum and phoney reverence perpetrated on the sensitive section of the public for a very long time. Great hosts of extras have been hired to charge across the giant screen, Gina Lollobrigida has been asked - and consented - to take a bath and both Yul Brynner and George Sanders spend much time striding round with odd-looking helmets on their heads. Few films have had battle scenes so gory and furious as this. They are the only snatches of valuable cinema in nearly $2^1/_2$ hours of Biblical boredom.

'It was the quietest New Year's Eve Brighton's ever seen,' reported the Brighton and Hove Gazette in its first January edition of the new decade. 'As church bells rang in 1960 a steady drizzle of rain fell, and the only people in sight were a handful of policemen and a couple buying a hot-dog on the windswept seafront. At the Corn Exchange 1,200 dancers celebrated the biggest ball in the town. In a basket full of balloons, eighteen-year-old Joan Hammond emerged as 'Miss Sport 1960' at the Brighton Co-operative Hall. When all the dances ended and the pubs closed a few tired revellers sang, someone did a Highland reel on a street corner and there was a bit of rock and roll on another. Brighton police reported: 'No incidents, it's been fairly quiet.' At Hove there were 'just one or two worse for drink.'

News events of the 1960s began on a similarly downbeat note with the last of Brighton's fishermen, seen below, being forced to move - in January - from their fish market building on the seafront. This was between the piers, where they had been since the 1860s; they were to go to new premises in Circus Street, adjoining the town's fruit and vegetable market. This was completely against their wishes and huge ill-feeling was directed at the Corporation (as the Council was referred to then), who had stated their old market building was smelly, unhygienic and out of date.

Heritage matters were well to the fore at this time. The town was still reeling from the demolition of St Margaret's Church, seen below, the previous year. This stood in St Margaret's Place, off Cannon Place, and was opened on Boxing Day, 1824, so was actually one of the few genuinely Georgian churches in Brighton. It had a unique domed roof and from inside resembled a miniature St Paul's Cathedral. In time it became one of the most popular churches in Brighton for the wealthy, but due to its proximity to the seafront, a special gallery was provided for Brighton's fishermen and their families.

The last service had been in September 1956 and it was demolished in preparation for redeveloping a large site behind the Metropole Hotel, where exhibition halls, an underground car park and the 24-storey Sussex Heights flats would later be built. This project features a great deal in the pages which follow.

In January, the pantomime 'Puss In Boots' continued a seasonal run at the Hippodrome, described as 'a fun-packed show; the type of

production that should keep pantomime alive forever.' The stars were Arthur Haynes, Freddie Sales and Joy Turpin. Another Christmas show at this time was the skating spectacle 'Humpty Dumpty', at the Palladium ice rink, which is the name the SS Brighton in West Street was operating under at the start of the 1960s (new owners - the Rank Organisation

- had taken over in 1959). This is seen opposite. 'Some of the colour ensembles were magnificent,' reported the local press, 'right from the King's Horses - who wiggled when they walked - through to the colourful inferno scene and to the last grand finale. Never have we seen a more evil witch than Joise Cordrey, or a more beautiful fairy than Lola Farrell. But best of all we liked Humpty himself - shapely Sue Park to you - vivacious, dainty and good to look at.'

However, an article about live shows in a January Brighton and Hove Gazette sounded a prophetic note, with its headline; 'Hippodrome About To Drop Variety?' It commented that the theatre didn't have one variety show booked between now and Easter. Manager Angus Franklin stated: 'The only variety bills we will get are the very top attractions like Bruce Forsyth and Max Bygraves.' 'Variety fans better stick to television,' the article concluded, 'because the chances of seeing their favourite 'turns' in Brighton or anywhere else are very slim.' Time would prove him right.

January saw the start of work on building a subway from the bottom of West Street, under King's Road and out onto the lower promenade.

In February 1960 came news that a printing works of books for the blind, situated in Queen's Road, was about to move to Reigate. This was the Moon Society's works, something of a Brighton institution, established over a hundred years previously by Dr William Moon, pioneer of an embossed type, similar to Braille, but with larger and simpler characters. Administered by the Royal National Institute for the Blind, a huge range of material using this type was generated at the Queen's Road works and distributed all over the world. The building itself was well known as it too was literally 'blind' - no windows faced Queen's Road - and was always covered in posters and advertisements. The view here shows it coming down early in 1961. The new building on the site would, it was stated, 'further enhance Queen's Road as Brighton's growing commercial centre.'

At the same time in Queen's Road a large site between North Road and Church Street was going to be redeveloped as well. Churchill House, at the southern corner of North Street, was about to be demolished, its owners, the Eagle Star insurance group, intending to replace it with a five-storey office block.

Churchill House was opened after World War II by Sir Winston Churchill as an ex-serviceman's club and was bought with money raised through what was known as Brighton's 'Thank You' fund. After only a few years though, the club was wound up and the building sold for office use.

Another, near the northern corner of Church Street, was occupied by the curiously named Odd Fellows Hall. The Odd Fellows were a charitable, fraternal organisation, providing mutual aid for those who were members as well as help for the poor and needy of their area. Churchill House and the Odd Fellows Hall are both seen below, left and right respectively.

Most sources state the first Odd Fellow groups were operating in London during the 1740s; the unusual name probably coming from the widely differing, 'odd' trades of the members that formed the first groups. The building in Queen's Road, housing a Brighton branch, was built by a John Fabian, in 1853, through donations and fund-raising. The foundation stone - still in place on the office block that occupies the site today - was laid by the Chief Constable of Brighton, H. B. Tamplin. He must be connected with Tamplins, the well-known local brewers somewhere along the line. The hall was officially opened in June 1854.

The hall is best remembered as the location for medicals for men about to serve in World War II. These were pretty embarrassing - some of the recruits were just seventeen years old - particularly when it was a female doctor doing the examining! The check up was very basic: a specimen had to be produced, then, 'bend over', 'cough', 'can you hear what I'm whispering to you?' etc., plus the reading of an eye chart. There was an aptitude test afterwards that involved taking a door lock apart and fitting it together again, then a test involving arithmetic and basic writing skills.

Once the NHS was set up, after the war, the Odd Fellows role in assisting with health care and funerals was obviously reduced, but other support work continued. The Brighton building was sold off for redevelopment - quite why is the only part of the story that's still a mystery. Some old shops in between Churchill House and the Odd Fellows Hall were also cleared and typical 1960s offices eventually covered the whole eastern side of Queen's Road, from Church Street to North Road.

One interesting tit-bit of 1960 information was when the Borough Engineer and Surveyor, D J Howe, reported that a police survey of February revealed there were 2853 cars on Brighton's streets at this time. He estimated than in six years time, this number could be 6000!

Teenagers and coffee bars drifted in and out of the news a great deal during the decade. In a Brighton and Hove Gazette of March 1960, a girl named Joy - in a piece headed 'The teenagers' point of view' - stated: 'Parents should not forbid their children to go to coffee-bars as this, rather than preventing teen-agers from visiting such places, only leads to lies and mistrust between parents and children. I know of the trouble that occasionally occurs in coffee-bars, but I also know of the fights in the streets, in public houses and in dance-halls. But because coffee-bars are a comparatively new attraction and are frequented by teen-agers they are always news. If a fight starts in one, or even near one, it is bound to be in the newspapers the next day. The result is the coffee-bar gets a bad name and the parents of many teen-agers forbid their off-spring to go there any more.'

She went on, 'There are hundreds of teen-agers who are bored and want to come out and enjoy themselves - to sit, to drink coffee, to jive and to meet people. If more youth clubs broadened their outlook and opened premises with this type of modern background then I doubt if the coffee-bars would be frequented every night so much as they are. Good luck to the coffee-bars and the dance halls that cater for teen-agers and to the parents who understand their children and trust them to be sensible.'

Entertainment during early March included the musical 'Salad Days' at the Hippodrome, 'The Billy Barnes Revue' at the Theatre Royal, the film *Anatomy of Murder* at the Curzon, with *Two Way Stretch* at the Astoria. Top Rank Dancing was at the Regent (Rank owned the Regent at this time), with wrestling at the Palladium. At Easter, Julia Lockwood (daughter of Margaret Lockwood, the film star) played Peter Pan, with Richard Wordsworth as Captain Hook.

One large preoccupation for the Corporation throughout the first half of the 1960s was the Albion Hill Redevelopment Scheme, as it was officially known, estimated (initially) to cost a million pounds. This project will be revisited several times as the decade proceeds. Basically it involved rebuilding - and relandscaping - a huge area between Edward Street and Albion Hill that until the late 1920s was a labyrinth of tightly packed slum streets, courtyards and alleyways. Many were cleared from 1928 onwards, with some rebuilding in the 1930s (the Tarner estate, plus the Milner and Kingswood flats) but the area remained largely derelict as the 1960s began, due mainly to World War II holding rebuilding work up. The aerial photograph here, taken in 1960, shows about half the site, with many streets standing devoid of buildings. At the very top of the view one of the high-rise blocks of flats that now dominate the area is under construction.

Back in January 1958, the Brighton and Hove Herald had the first detailed description of the scheme and it's interesting to see how high-rise redevelopment was 'sold' to the public then:

'The first stage in the creation of a pleasant vista from the Queen's Park Road ridge down the valley to St Peter's Church is likely to be commenced next September. In the process, a mass of old houses now huddled together will be swept away, and in their places will appear blocks of flats, some of the 'skyscraper' variety.

This ambitious transformation plan takes in just over eleven acres. On this extremely hilly ground it has been decided to erect 426 dwellings in 'mixed development'; that is to say in 2,3,8 and 11-storey blocks.

The first stage envisages that 144 flats in 2,3 and 8-storey blocks on an area of 33.3 acres, bounded by Albion Street, Richmond Street, Albion Hill and Cambridge Street.

The whole scheme - which is under the direction of the Borough Engineer and Surveyor (Mr D J Howe), with Mr P Billington as Chief Architect - was approved by the Planning Committee some time ago. It has this week passed the Housing Committee, and will come before the Town Council shortly.

The creation of a self-contained community in the heart of modern Brighton is the object in view, for it is intended to incorporate in the new estate shops and social amenities, together with provision for religious activities.

Club and community centre provision will probably be made possible in semi-basements of the taller buildings.

Health-giving open spaces, for so long absent from this close-packed, hilly area, will lead through the estate right up to the ridge of Queen's Park Road.

'Every effort has been made to accommodate as many people in light, airy and modern blocks of flats as are at present

accommodated in the slum conditions now prevailing here,' Councillor A J M Johnson, chairman of the Housing Committee told the Herald yesterday. 'This is necessary,' he said,' in order to avoid overspill, which would occur if the area were redeveloped in terraced housing.

By the use of high blocks of flats it has been possible to provide large areas of open space surrounding the blocks which will be planted with trees and grass.'

'The old people have not been overlooked; they will be housed in the 2 and 3-storey blocks in the lower portions of the estate.

Owing to the contours of the ground the taller blocks of flats will have semi-basement areas, where accommodation for drying areas and bin stores will be provided. The higher blocks will have lifts.

A widened carriageway up Richmond Street will give the main approach to the new estate.'

The view on the opposite page shows the 'Thornsdale' flats almost finished. Mayor Alan Johnson officially opened the building in May 1961.

In April 1960, the Corporation stated that post-war slum clearance in Brighton, started in 1955, had almost reached the halfway mark. 1016 families had had their properties condemned; 872 had now been rehoused, with plans for a further 934 to be accommodated. 'By next September,' the local press was told, 'it is hoped that the four new skyscraper blocks in Albion Hill, replacing Cambridge Street and Albion Street, will be ready for 180 families to move in.' In fact six blocks, not four, were eventually built.

Another substantial project, adjoining the Albion Hill site, but separate to it, was for a new Police Station and Law Court building for derelict John Street, off Edward Street, replacing a much smaller police HQ near the Town Hall. The architectural model for this is seen opposite. In fact there was much debate about whether a new Town Hall itself should be built as part of the development. A new town hall for Brighton had been put forward, on and off, since the 1930s, as the one in Bartholomews, dating from 1830-31, had been too small from the start to house all the various local government departments under one roof. This plan would crop up again in 1961.

Yet another redevelopment site was making headlines early in 1960 when a two-day public enquiry was held into the future of the Blackman Street area (between Trafalgar Street and Cheapside). Houses here had been condemned as slums by Brighton's Medical Officer, Dr. W. S. Parker, who said they were

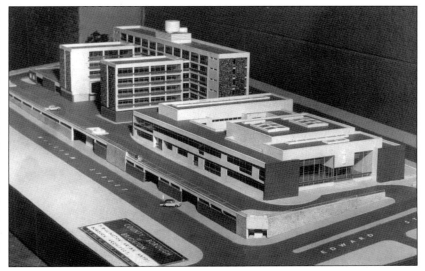

'old, worn-out, damp and in need of repair'. But a huge row flared up during the course of the enquiry as Wood Street, Redcross Street and Whitecross Street had also been declared slums and hastily - it seemed - added to the list of those that would be compulsorily purchased. The Corporation was accused of 'land grabbing' and getting a much bigger area to redevelop than was previously thought. Whitecross Street, it transpired, was to be cleared and widened to sixty feet for a new relief road through whatever development the area would take, running parallel with London Road from Trafalgar Street to New England Road. A lot of hot air was generated at the enquiry, with Dr Parker announcing he would stand down if subjected to any personal attacks from residents of the threatened streets; virtually everything was eventually demolished anyway (some in the 1970s) and the massive, nineteen-storey Theobald House and surrounding car park now dominates the whole site, opening in 1966. This is seen under construction here in 1965.

On a much smaller scale, the building seen below, the Albemarle Hotel, was coming down. It stood on a prominent seafront site, between Steine Street (left) and Manchester Street (right) and what amazed everyone - and still

does - was that nothing was built on the site for ten years. With most of Brighton seemingly being redeveloped on all sides the gap in the line of buildings at this point along Marine Parade would remain empty for the entire decade.

Some major stars were appearing in the Hippodrome's 1960 summer show, 'Let's Be Happy'. Frankie Vaughan topped the bill, supported by Tommy Cooper, Roy Castle and singer Adele Lee. There was also Summer Masquerade at the Essoldo, with Cyril Fletcher, Craig Douglas and Eric Delaney and his band. The spectacular 'Hot Ice' featured at the Palladium. On the Palace Pier, the Forbes Russell repertory company presented a season of popular plays. Films showing at this time included the musical *Gigi* at the Curzon, *The Last Days of Pompeii* at the Regent, plus *Around The World In Eighty Days* at the Gaiety, Lewes Road. At the Ritz, bingo sessions were now on offer. In August, the great Alfred Hitchcock shocker, *Psycho,* played the Odeon in West Street.

On - or under - the West Pier during the summer of 1960, Brighton's own Great Omani (in reality Ron Cunningham) could be found performing various stunts and escapes in the great tradition of past seaside performers. He's seen here 'driving' a speedboat under the pier, blindfolded. He's set the sea alight too, just to complicate things!

The Hotel Metropole was about to lose its central rooftop spire in September 1960. This was part of the original 1890 building and became something of a seafront landmark. The press reported: 'Part of the copper covering was heard banging about in the wind recently, the whole spire was examined and it was decided to remove it.' A spokesman for the owners - AVP Industries said: 'We decided the whole structure was dangerous and so it has come down. It was a decision we were very reluctant to take, but it was a matter of public safety.'

Cynical comments were made about the owners wanting to get rid of the spire just so they could enlarge the hotel by building more accommodation on the roof (which they did), all part of the wider plan to upgrade the hotel; details of the new exhibition halls and an underground car park were being finalised at this time.

September 1960 was also the month when the Minister of Housing and Local Government approved the demolition of several houses in Waterloo Place, opposite the bottom of the Level, for the construction of an office building. The terrace, part of which is seen here, was built about 1819 by Brighton's celebrated architects Amon Wilds and Amon Henry Wilds and formed one of the most attractive Regency properties in the whole town. Originally, it was made up of fourteen separate houses. The decision was the beginning of the end for the whole terrace as eventually, apart from no's 1 and 2, the whole line of houses was lost and replaced by Wellesley House in 1968-70. One house, no 9, where pensioner Harriet Sylvester wouldn't sell up, nor could be forced to, meant the new office building went up in two sections, with her house in between. On her death, in 1974, it was removed and the gap treated to make one continuous building.

On the outskirts of the town, November 1960 saw the 700th anniversary of St Peter's Church, Preston. Its ancient history was recalled by the Brighton and Hove Herald including some supernatural occurrences: 'In its long history', it continued, 'St Peter's has not been without its share of ghosts. There are records of apparitions appearing as far back as 1535. Mostly the perturbed spirits have been seen in the apparel of a nun. In 1897 a skeleton of a woman, said to be 400 years old, was found in a corner of the Manor and was subsequently interred in the churchyard. Frequently up until that time an apparition of a 'woman in white' had been seen walking in the vicinity, but after the skeleton had been given a Christian burial the figure was no longer seen.'

The paper also drew readers' attention to the ancient wall frescoes, which Henry VIII had ordered to be covered over, as they depicted the martyrdom of Thomas More; following restoration in 1830, they formed something of a tourist attraction. They were mostly lost in a fire of June 1906 and only a few fragments survived; the paper didn't mention that the blaze was started by choirboys, sneakily smoking cigarettes!

Sherrys Bar and the Ritz Skating Rink in West Street are seen in December 1960, a forlorn shadow of their illustrious past. It was of course, from 1918, the legendary Sherrys Dance Hall, which along with the Regent in Queen's Road, was where a whole generation of Brighton residents and visitors danced away their youth. It became a key location in Graham Greene's notorious book, *Brighton Rock,* which shocked the town when first published in 1938, as did the later 1947 film. Sherrys was at the height of its popularity during World War II, when it was packed every night (as was the Regent) with all nationalities of allied service personnel. It closed in September 1948 (actually reopening for another year or so), but eventually succumbed to being a roller-skating rink (as here), then a bingo hall (6d a game), the same as several other well-known entertainment buildings in the town during the 1960s. The front of the building would come down early in 1969 and the interior revamped as a Mississippi-style saloon bar; several different nightclubs have subsequently occupied the site, so the dancing continues - albeit very different dancing.

The year closed with two main seasonal shows. The pantomime at the Hippodrome was 'Dick Whittington' with Charlie Chester; 'Sleeping Beauty' was at the Palladium ice rink in West Street, with guest stars the Kaye Sisters. The musical 'Salad Days' was at the Theatre Royal. Four full-sized theatres were operating in central Brighton in 1960. These were the Theatre Royal in New Road, the Essoldo in North Street, the Hippodrome in Middle Street and the theatre on the Palace Pier.

At the Regent in Queen's Road and at the Aquarium ballroom, dancing sessions were being held virtually every night.

The Regent cinema was showing Disney's *Pollyanna*, the Astoria had the Cole Porter musical *Can Can*, with more Disney at the Continental, where *Cinderella* was playing with *Old Yeller*.

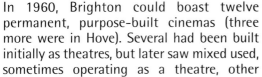

In 1960, Brighton could boast twelve permanent, purpose-built cinemas (three more were in Hove). Several had been built initially as theatres, but later saw mixed used, sometimes operating as a theatre, other times as cinema. Alphabetically, these were the Academy in West Street, the Astoria in Gloucester Place, the Continental at Kemp Town, the Curzon in Western Road, the Duke of York's at Preston Circus, the Essoldo in North Street (above right), the Gaiety in Lewes Road, the Odeon in West Street, another Odeon in St George's Road, Kemp Town, The Paris in New Road, the Princes News Theatre in North Street (which became the Jacey in 1966), the Regent in Queen's Road (above left), plus the Savoy in East Street (becoming the ABC in early 1961). Some would change name as the decade progressed. Before World War II there had been *eighteen* cinemas. Due mainly to the impact of TV, a number would close during the 1960s (the Kemp Town Odeon was the first casualty, going in November 1960 and becoming a bingo hall in 1962); in 2006, only one cinema from the whole list remains operating - the Duke of York's - with virtually all the others demolished. The 1960s was not a good decade for cinemas in Brighton or anywhere else for that matter. Due mainly to the rise in TV ownership, attendance figures nationally dwindled from 500 million in 1960 to 215 million in 1969.

1961

Some Key Events:

January	- The millionth BMC Morris Minor car came off the production line. Gerry Anderson's 'Supercar' first seen on TV.
February	- Footballer Danny Blanchflower famously refuses to appear on the TV show 'This Is Your Life.'
March	- The Beatles make their first appearance at the Cavern club in Liverpool.
April	- Russian Major Yuri Gagarin becomes the first man to orbit the earth.
June	- A Census puts the population of Britain at 52,675,094.
August	- The Berlin Wall is started between East and West Berlin.
September	- The first 'Mothercare' shop opens in Kingston, South London.
October	- James Hanratty arrested for A6 murder.
November	- The government announces it will introduce an immigration bill.
December	- The first US soldier is killed in the Vietnam War (James Davis).

No 1 in the music charts at Christmas was 'Moon River' by Danny Williams

Social Snippets: The BBC play *Cathy Come Home* (shown in December 1961), caused a huge stir in Britain and the plight of the homeless became a major social issue. The charity 'Shelter' was subsequently formed.

Also in 1961, the contraceptive pill first became available in the UK, initially to married women only, two years later to unmarried women. Contraception involving injections, effective for a month, were also available for a while, but subsequently banned.

Local Film Review: *Ben-Hur* (shown at Astoria)

As sheer entertainment, *Ben-Hur* is the nearest you'll ever get to a Roman holiday for five shillings. The chariot race, which is the film's high spot, is the most exciting thing I've ever seen on the screen. A man who has seen the film three times tells me, with a trace of surprise, that each time he has watched the race the same team of horses won. But perhaps - next time...That's how realistic the race is! Just as realistic are some of the other gory episodes. Galley slaves are flogged, a Macedonian pirate has a flaming torch thrust painfully into his face in the huge sea battle scene, and at the Crucifixion a soldier hammers home the nails most convincingly. If this last is unnecessarily gruesome - and I think it is - it will also give Christians the shock that many of them need.

In the very first Brighton and Hove Herald of January 1961 came intriguing speculation of building a yachting harbour at Brighton. Not at Black Rock, where the Marina would eventually take shape in the 1970s, but at the Banjo Groyne, which was to be enlarged and extended, by curving it eastwards, parallel with the shore, creating a protective harbour wall. The entrance, some 175' wide, would be from the east. The cost of the project was estimated at £40,000, including a car park, and would take twenty-one months to build.

Dennis Howe, Brighton's Borough Surveyor, had said, 'There is no doubt that the construction of a harbour would be welcomed in many quarters', and consultants confirmed that the Banjo Groyne was ideal as a foundation for an offshore backwater. Amazingly, a site further east, at Black Rock (where the Marina would eventually be built) was rejected as 'unsuitable'. The Royal Yachting Association thought the plan was too small, saying; 'wave action would damage vessels lying at moorings in rough weather'. Brighton's Deep Sea Anglers group and the Brighton Sailing Club, both welcomed the scheme, but the sailing club thought the car parking charges - 10/6d a day - were far too high.

How quickly this idea came and went; by the end of January, the plan had been scrapped.

Anyone thinking of booking up for a holiday in early 1961 would find plenty of choice among the advertisements in January's local papers. Thomas Cook, then in North Street were offering a two-week Austrian trip, by air, for £37/12/-; an eight-day rail trip to Nice, France, for £25/14/-; fifteen days at Alassio, Italy for £31/1/-; fifteen days at the Costa Brava for £31/1/- and a week, by air, to Lucerne, Switzerland for £30/14/-. A trip to Canada on the SS Homeric, sailing from Southampton had prices starting from £62. The average weekly wage in Britain was now £15/10/-, so these prices would have seemed pretty reasonable to most people then. The traditional week or two-week seaside holiday, once an established feature of British life, was being severely challenged by this sort of alternative.

Fashion was well to the fore too. Nancy Gray, compiler of the 'Specially For Women' page in the Brighton and Hove Herald, gave her 'pet hates' regarding current fashion trends in a January edition:

'Winkle pickers that make feet look like canal barges and are chiropodists' delights ('When they're 40 they'll be hobbling around like a Chinese woman who's had bound feet!').

Above-knee (how knobbly some of them are!), figure-hugging-walk-preventing skirts.

Uncombed, unwashed 'bee-hives' of tousled tresses, vaguely reminiscent of Zulu styles'.

'Forgive me', she continued, 'if this sounds a bit like being a kill-joy. I'm anything but really...only sad when lovely young creatures in the first flush of their tempting girlhood make themselves hideous. Judicious make-up is lovely; heavy black-ringed eyes in a 16 or 17-year old face devoid of any colour is too much for me'.

Near the end of her feature (a whole page in the paper) ran an item headed 'Bye-Bye To The Beehive', where a leading hairdresser announced the beehive hair-do was a short-lived craze and definitely on its way out (wrong!).

In early February retired boxer Freddie Mills (often seen around Brighton and Hove) opened a new TV store in St James's Street. This was the Visda Showroom, proudly boasting in its advertisements to be -'first with the 19-inch TV'. A veteran of ninety-six fights, Mills was Light Heavyweight Champion of the World between 1948 and 1950 and appeared in a number of films including *Carry On Constable* (1959) and *Saturday Night Out* (a 1963 film starring pop group *The Searchers*). He died in July 1965, supposedly having shot himself.

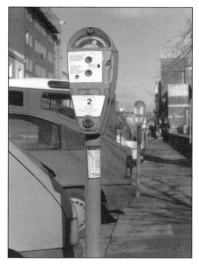

Plans for a new Town Hall were being hotly debated in the early 1960s, to replace the old one in Bartholomews. Similar deliberations had been held on and off for decades. By the spring of 1961, it was thought an ideal site would definitely be in Edward Street, but as one interested individual said at this time: 'The new Town hall should be built on rollers so that it can be pushed around until its location is finally agreed!'

In fact Edward Street was in the news a great deal at this time as plans were being finalised to complete a widening programme actually begun in the late 1920s and abandoned during World War II. This had resulted in a huge bottleneck being left from George Street eastwards. The new police station would be built off the northern side and St John's School in Carlton Hill enlarged; seven acres of redevelopment in all. It was said to be 'the biggest civic development in Brighton of the century', and apart from the Town Hall, everything planned for the development actually went ahead. However, extending the new roadway into Kemp Town, later in the decade, would be an entirely different matter.

'Whole Centre of Brighton in the M Zone', announced a Brighton and Hove Gazette of April 1961. This was the headline for an article detailing reaction to plans for installing parking meters in the town centre. The picture above shows some in New Road, many years after they began operating. Back in 1961, the main justification for meters was seen as improving traffic flow by eliminating haphazard parking. It continued: 'Opposition to Brighton's Watch Committee's sweeping parking meter plans hardened yesterday as traders, businessmen and residents began to realise the full implications of the scheme to turn the main business and shopping centre of the town into a meter zone.' The 'zone' was basically the rectangle bordered by King's Road, Old Steine, Pavilion Parade, Church Street, Upper North Street, part of Western Road, Upper North Street, Hampton Place and Preston Street.

1093 meters were proposed, at a cost of £44,000, with 40 traffic wardens employed at salaries between £595 and £665 per year (the one seen here was photographed directing traffic in Gloucester Road in 1966). It was estimated the plan would make a profit of £23,200 a year.

'There will be five new 'crimes' if the meter scheme is adopted,' the paper advised, somewhat tongue in cheek. 'It will be an offence to park at a meter without paying; to park anywhere else in the zone except at a meter; to park at a meter already occupied; to park across two meter spaces; and to stop in a goods loading bay.' And it announced the fine for any transgression of these new strictures would be a hefty £2, which sounds nothing now, but in 1961 seemed draconian. The meters would be in operation from 8 am to 8 pm, seven days a week on the sea front, but weekdays only for other areas. Two hours maximum parking time was allowed in the town, at a cost of 6d per half hour or 1/- for an hour. On the seafront it would be 2/- for four hours rising to 4/- for a maximum of eight hours parking.

Those against the scheme pointed out that a third of parking spaces would be lost because the size of the new bays would have to be some 18-20 ft in length to accommodate large cars - and two smaller cars would not be allowed in one space. One of the fiercest opponents was Councillor Stanley Theobald (Theobald House was named after him) who said: 'I shall fight this tooth and nail. I would have thought our job was to look after the people of Brighton and not one of them has asked for anything like this scheme. It is more important that trade is done in these roads than that people should be able to hurry through. I am afraid parking meters will make this a dead centre. Hove and other areas where parking is easier will get the benefit out of what Brighton is doing.' Whatever the opposition, parking meters began operating in Brighton during March 1963 - with the number of them increased to 1180!

In May 1961, the ballroom at the Aquarium was being converted into a museum for period motor vehicles. This would prove a popular attraction for a number of years, but would later become the area where a large dolphin pool would be constructed in 1968.

An old theatre, the Grand in North Road, was gutted by a spectacular fire in June 1961. It was redundant as a theatre at this time, and being used as a furniture factory owned by the firm of Bevan-Funnell; the managing director was Barry Funnell, who had only relinquished his post as Mayor of Hove a week before. 'There was a noise like gunfire as the roof crashed in,' stated the Brighton and Hove Herald in its report. Sixty firemen from Brighton, Hove, Southwick and Lewes 'fought to control flames which leaped more than eighty feet into the sky and a watch was kept on adjoining property as flaming brands showered over a wide area.'

The theatre had opened way back in October 1891 as the New Hippodrome Circus (nothing to do with the

Hippodrome in Middle Street), with room for over 5000 spectators, making it the biggest theatrical venue in Brighton. Two strange acts seen on opening night were Mephisto, a contortionist, known as 'the boneless wonder', and Professor Frederick's miniature circus of performing cats, rats, mice and monkeys. One monkey climbed a rope to the ceiling then jumped and floated down on a tiny parachute.

In 1894 the Circus became a conventional theatre, the Eden, and was the place to see sensational melodramas. Plays involving murder, suicide, robberies, duelling, shipwrecks, earthquakes, trains colliding, explosions and general mayhem, 'packed them in', as did the annual pantomime, with its spectacular scenery and effects. The theatre became the Grand in 1904, but the full-bloodied fare remained the same, particularly when local man Andrew Melville owned it, from 1922 to 1931. Variety and even nude shows were mixed into the heady brew served up at the Grand, but audiences dwindled when 'talkie' cinemas began to open up in the area. The Grand became a cinema itself from January 1931, with a brief return to live variety during World War II. The Grand closed down in February 1955 (seen here) and served as a furniture store for a number of years, before burning down. The remains were cleared shortly afterwards and an office block was eventually built on the site.

It was the end of another era too when in early July 1961, the last trolley bus ran in Brighton. They'd started operating in May 1939 and replaced the trams, which had run since 1901. This last one left its depot in Lewes Road at 11.30 and made a short tour of the town before going to the breakers yard. Trolley buses were powered by an overhead series of electric wires, which were eventually difficult to manoeuvre through the town's increasingly heavy traffic and double-parked vehicles. During their operation though, it was estimated the 25 buses that operated had carried 465 million passengers covering a collective distance of some 35 million miles!

In July 1961 a homeless family were found living in a tent on the Level - real-life shades of 'Cathy Come Home'. The story was reported in the Brighton and Hove Herald: 'Mr Frederick Ancell, a 23-year-old hod carrier, his pretty 20-year-old wife Carol and their eight months old son, have been unable to find anywhere to live since they were evicted from their unfurnished flat in Trafalgar Street when the property was bought by a development company some months ago. They had been living at Mr Ancell's

father's house in Whitehawk Crescent but it was overcrowded, and on Monday they left to set up home on the Level. Mr Ancell has taken time off work to be with his wife, and his firm are supporting him. 'I know there'll always be a job for me when I go back - they are 100 per cent behind me.' A spokesman for Brighton Housing Department said: 'The chairman is being kept informed about this case which will come up before the committee on Thursday. At the last 10 committee meetings we have dealt with 266 cases of this type and 132 have been passed.' This presumably meant resolved. 'We don't see any reason for taking exceptional action in this case.'

July 1961 brought news of a plan for redeveloping an extremely large area bounded by Western Road, West Street, King's Road and Cannon Place. This would eventually become the site for the Churchill Square shopping centre, car parks and Top Rank Entertainment centre. Sixteen plans had been prepared for this area in 1959 (two are seen here) and by the early sixties these had been whittled down to three. Sir Hugh Casson, the distinguished architect, responsible for some of the Festival of Britain's most celebrated buildings the previous decade, had been called in as chief consultant for all the town's main redevelopment schemes. 'Don't be afraid of high buildings,' Sir Hugh advised the Council, but added that none should exceed 160 ft and anything this size should be mainly grouped between the piers.

'The subtopian mess of lamp-standards and road signs' at the Aquarium roundabout should be replanned, so that when visitors get their first glimpse of the sea, it should be 'a setting - strong, clean and simple - worthy of the occasion.' The Lanes he regarded as 'Brighton's Kasbah', where the heart of the Old Town was still preserved and 'bursting with vitality.' Vehicles should be kept out, he advised, and arcades and pedestrian shopping lanes should be developed.

Specifically on the area that would become Churchill Square, Sir Hugh thought the area around Grenville Place (first street south of Western Road) 'needs particularly sensitive handling, and St Paul's Church, - one of the finest of its period in the country - should not be ignored, but be properly integrated into the new plan.' Sensitive handling was the last thing it got, with Grenville Place demolished (some of its houses are seen on the next page), with part of Clarence Square also cleared and St Paul's not integrated at all, becoming just a peripheral survivor.

Sir Hugh did warn though that seaside towns like Brighton should keep their individuality. 'If we are not careful,' he said, 'soon we will

not be able to tell Bournemouth from Eastbourne or Blackpool from Brighton.'

But back to the plan for redeveloping the site between Western Road and the seafront; the area of the 1961 version was now 15 acres (it had been 11½) and involve the southern side of Western Road (which it hadn't before) where an extensive new shopping centre would be built - this would become Churchill Square. Startlingly though, the demolition of the Grand Hotel was seriously contemplated; none of the 1950s plans envisaged this, but the hotel was suddenly included as part of the site. Sir Hugh Casson wanted the Grand to stay, describing it as 'splendid and spiffing'. If it went, it would mean the loss of everything in the entire area except St Paul's Church in West Street. On Grand Hotel site, a huge entertainment centre was visualized, featuring a dance hall, bowling alley, restaurant and conference facilities (for up to 4000 people) to allow bigger assemblies than those at the Dome, which held 2000 people and where most conferences took place at this time. An underground car park would accommodate between 2500 and 3000 vehicles. It really was a case of watch this space, for within a week or two the area involved had been extended even further to 16½ acres and now included three skyscraper blocks - one on King's Road at 350 ft tall, another at the rear of the Odeon Cinema 240 ft high and a third facing Cannon Place at 220 ft high. The model above shows these with the Grand Hotel 'erased'. It was thought the whole scheme would take Taylor Woodrow - the appointed construction team - five years to build.

Summer entertainment in Brighton was mainly Bernard Delfont's 'Summer Show of 1961' at the Hippodrome starring Russ Conway, Alfred Marks and Janie Marden, the ice show, 'Snow White and the Seven Dwarfs' was at the Palladium, while on the Palace Pier, the Forbes Russell Repertory Company returned to stage weekly plays, such as *Doctor In The House*. 'Tuesday at the Dome' was a popular, regular weekly variety show hosted by Douglas Reeve, featuring many local artists. The film *101 Dalmatians* was being shown at the Odeon.

In July 1961 'The Adam Faith Show' played the Essoldo in North Street, which usually operated as a cinema. This wasn't a one-man pop concert, but a variety show with Faith, topping the bill. Later to become an iconic figure of the 1960s, the local press reported; 'He has a pleasing voice and it is most refreshing to be able to hear almost every word he sings. His choice of numbers on the opening night, was, for the most part, predictable - 'When Johnny Comes Marching Home Again', 'Easy Going Me' and 'Someone Else's Baby' and there was

BRIGHTON & HOVE
Brilliant and Beautiful

something new to him, 'I Could Write A Book' which was fitted to his style very effectively.' Faith is seen opposite.

Others in the show included comedian Jimmy Jewel, a singing group called The Honeys and rising star Larry Grayson, described as a 'young man with a bright future.'

By July 1961 the powers that be finally concluded any new Town Hall should actually be sited where the present one stood. 'And so the Council have come - by way of suggestions during the past thirty years to build it everywhere from Peacehaven to Shoreham - back where they began,' reported the local press, somewhat cynically.

But...stepping back from all these comings and goings; it's worth pausing to see just how Brighton saw itself as a tourist resort in the early part of the decade. A look at the town's publicity brochure for 1961 just about sums it all up. The girl seen on the cover must be a grandmother by now. It's a pretty hefty booklet, running to over a hundred pages, mostly full of adverts for hotels, guest houses and B&B establishments. But it also gives details of the attractions Brighton and Hove could offer visitors and it's fascinating to see how the 'image' promoted all those years ago compares to that of today - it's startlingly different.

'Why not take a Spring Holiday at Tulip-time,' suggests the welcome on the introductory page, 'or in the Autumn with 'Dr Brighton' away from the smog? Brighton and Hove are wonderful any time of year.'

The emphasis in 1961 is clearly on the conventional seaside holiday and the slightly fuzzy colour photographs in the brochure - state-of-the-art colour printing then - show families making sandcastles together, playing crazy golf or having fun in one of the seafront paddling pools. It's a vastly different Brighton being portrayed to that of the early twenty-first century.

However, its sporting facilities that are emphasised more than anything else and the fourteen-acre Brighton Sports Area, at Withdean, currently temporary home to Brighton and Hove Albion, is described as 'the finest open-air sports and athletic area outside London.' This staged all sorts of events then, including the Brighton Horse Show and the South of England Jumping Championships, plus rugby, cricket, netball, archery and basketball matches.

There were two swimming pools in Brighton in 1961 (others were in neighbouring Hove and Rottingdean): Black Rock open-air pool (which would be demolished in 1983), plus the indoor baths in North Road (replaced by the Prince Regent in 1979-80). 'Black Rock Pool is a veritable swimmers' paradise,' the brochure says. 'Here, in sparkling sea water, thoroughly filtered and sterilized, bathing may be experienced at its unequalled best.'

One huge sporting attraction that Brighton could boast four decades ago was ice hockey. The rink for this - seen on page 82 - was at the bottom of West Street, for years known as the SS Brighton, but in 1961 had been renamed the Palladium. This stadium was home to the famous Brighton Tigers team, national champions three times and as popular as their football counterparts, the Brighton and Hove Albion. This building's full story and demise are given further on.

THE BRIGHTON SPORTS ARENA

for details of
ATHLETIC MEETINGS
CLUB SPORTS
CRICKET
RUGBY
ARCHERY
NETBALL

Please apply to
PARKS SUPERINTENDENT
Moulsecoomb Place
BRIGHTON

★

Accommodation for Club Meetings and Dances

. . . . . . a venue for all Sports without an equal south of London

The Withdean Sportsman

Parties & Receptions. Full Catering Services

OPEN TO THE PUBLIC DURING NORMAL LICENSING HOURS

FOR DETAILS APPLY TO :—G. A. HUME, ROYAL YORK BUILDINGS, BRIGHTON, I. · Phone 29804

Brighton had both piers operating at this time, but only the Palace Pier was offering summer season entertainment. The motor museum, housed in the Aquarium building (today the SeaLife Centre) had just opened and even a waxworks could be found on the seafront, just round the corner from the Royal Albion Hotel. Of course the Royal Pavilion was still the town's key historical attraction, with the Lanes also highlighted as a place not to miss.

Nightclubs and discos didn't really exist in the early 1960s. Dancing took place in ballrooms to live music and Brighton's main dance hall was the Regent, in Queen's Road, located on top of the cinema of the same name. Both the cinema and the ballroom were owned by the Rank Organisation at this time. The Aquarium on the seafront also housed a ballroom and open-air dancing took place at the head of the Palace Pier on summer evenings. There was Tussaud's Waxworks too, on the seafront, by the Royal Albion Hotel, where visitors could mix with 'majesty and murder.'

And the cost of a stay at Brighton then? In the 1961 brochure, the really big hotels don't give their prices, but some of the smaller ones, like the Hotel Victoria, at the corner of King's Road and West Street, quote 10 to 12 guineas per person per week (a guinea would be £1.05 today). The Ellesmere Hotel, in New Steine, was 7-9 guineas per week, for full board, while Dorset House, in Dorset Gardens, offered bread and breakfast for £4 10s (£4.50 today) for a week in the summer. Prices were usually quoted in guineas as proprietors thought it gave their hotel or accommodation a touch of class. But notice how these prices compare with the foreign holiday costs given earlier.

Differentials were starting to close.

Those wanting a camping holiday would have to set up tent near East Brighton Park: 'Sheepcote Valley Camp nestles amid the glorious Sussex Downs, yet is less than a mile from the sea. It has every amenity for a perfect camping holiday readily to hand - hot and cold showers, modern toilets, a shop to supply your needs - these are just a few.'

Apart from a list of places of interest to visit around Brighton, like Arundel and Bramber, there isn't that much more on offer in Brighton's publicity brochure for 1961. It all seems a bit simple, even naïve now, but remember this was a time when package trips abroad were still in their infancy - and very costly, as we've already seen - and holidays 'at home' were much more the norm. In 1960, for example, Spain recorded only some six million visitors compared with fifty-two million in 1990. Also, attitudes and outlook were different and expectations weren't quite so high. The pace of life then was a lot more leisurely too. Many families didn't own cars and reliance on public transport was much more widespread than today. Coming to Brighton four decades ago would have been by train for most visitors, or by coach. Those who did come by car would have found hardly any parking restrictions compared with today - parking meters weren't introduced to Brighton until 1963 (and were just under 3p an hour!). And there were certainly no double yellow lines in the road to worry about.

One quote from the 1961 brochure's welcome page - 'At any time of the year the spirit of Brighton and Hove is alive and exciting - you will never have a dull moment.' - probably still rings true today.

But returning back to the main goings on of 1961...

In August the annual 'Miss Brighton' contest was held (at the Regent cinema) with a new rule introduced for competitors - they now had to be local girls and not 'outsiders'.

The American singer Johnny Mathis appeared at the Dome in August and in October, the popular 'Black and White Minstrel Show' would play the Hippodrome for a week.

In September it was announced that a new teacher training college would be built at Falmer for 500 trainees, to replace existing premises on the seafront at Kemp Town. It would be ready in four years' time.

One event of September that clouded the carefree wholesomeness of Brighton's image was when a sensational homicide, known as the Blue Gardenia murder, hit local and national headlines.

The owner of the Blue Gardenia nightclub in Queen Square, Harvey Holford, shot his wife Christine (formerly Christine Hughes, from Saltdean) in their flat above the club. This was all the more shocking as their marriage had only recently taken place in November 1960 at Dorset Gardens Methodist Church. Holford was reasonably wealthy and cultivated a playboy image, driving a red Pontiac Parisienne car, often with a speedboat in tow behind it, which he'd named the Christina. In May 1961 a daughter, Karen, was born, but while holidaying with the child's nanny in France, Christine met wealthy tycoon John Bloom, head of the Rolls Razor Company, who manufactured twin-tub washing machines. He dazzled Christine (he reputedly had twenty cars, three boats and a private plane) and in return for becoming his mistress, said he'd provide her with flats in Mayfair and Monte Carlo, plus £20,000 a year to live on. Christine - extremely naively - thought her husband might just accept this and use the money to buy property next door to his club, to replace the small top floor flat. Obviously this was definitely not acceptable to Harvey. Although she returned to him, tensions built up, their relationship became stormy and Christine, clearly obsessed with Bloom and his money, said she would be going back to him.

On 15th September 1961, police were alerted after a new nanny found bloodstains in the kitchen at the flat above the Blue Gardenia Club. They found the couple lying in bed; Christine had been shot six times and Holford was unconscious from an overdose. A gun was under the bed. He took three days to come round and was charged with Christine's murder. At the trial, held at Lewes Crown Court, the prosecution built up a picture of a jealous husband, meticulously planning the murder and coolly carrying it out. However, when the defence unravelled the story of Christine's infatuation with Bloom, how the overdose was a suicide attempt and how Holford kept a gun for his own protection, the jury clearly believed this was a crime of passion and Holford received a three-year manslaughter sentence. He was given parole in October 1964. He lived in Brighton under another name and died quite recently. Bloom's washing machine empire subsequently went bankrupt in 1964.

October also saw a really fiery, day-long inquiry at the Town Hall, where the £85,000 plan for making Edward Street a dual carriageway, mentioned in the introduction to this book, was debated. It was agreed that Edward Street was a hotchpotch of widths at this time (only 15 ft in one section) and that properties on its northern side - up to Tillstone Street - would have to be compulsorily purchased - to even up the width and continue the widening eastwards. It was envisaged that the final width would be 64 ft, and a full dual carriageway created. Even at this meeting though, no one, it seems, was saying where the dual carriageway was going to end. All the focus was on the Edward Street section and traffic flow at the western end, where it would turn south into Pavilion Parade opposite the Royal Pavilion. It was envisaged that 'very terrifying' traffic problems would be created at this junction. The ease of ambulances getting to the Royal Sussex

County Hospital was one positive aspect pointed up (they were invariably using Marine Parade), but again, no-one was seeing the bottleneck they'd hit, where Edward Street meets Eastern Road. It's a problem the area is still bogged down in today.

In October, the Royal Fine Art Commission objected to the demolition of houses in Grand Parade, scheduled to be cleared for the main building of a new art college complex, to replace the existing 1860s one, seen here. This caused a hold-up for a while, but the properties concerned eventually came down.

In December, the Council's Housing Committee reported, that Liverpool Street, Dinapore Street (running off bottom left in the view opposite), Richmond Street (diagonally right) and Albion Hill still had many houses 'unfit for human habitation' to be cleared and 145 people would subsequently need rehousing. These would eventually be cleared as part of the Albion Hill scheme, despite a public inquiry being held to determine their fate.

Seasonal shows in December 1961 included Jimmy Edwards in 'The Pied Piper' at the Hippodrome, while 'Sooty's Christmas Party' could be seen the week before Christmas at the Theatre Royal. Films included *Babes In Toyland* at the Odeon, *In The Doghouse* at the Regent, *King of Kings* at the Astoria and *The Magic Boy* at the Academy.

The year ended with the cheerful news that the number of parking meters in the town centre would now be 1246!

1962

Some Key Events:

January	- The Beatles audition for Decca records - and fail to get a deal.
February	- James Hanratty receives the death sentence for the A6 murder.
April	- 'Panda' push-button crossings introduced in Britain.
May	- The new Coventry Cathedral consecrated. Designed by Basil Spence.
July	- Telstar, the communications satellite is launched.
August	- Death of Marilyn Monroe.
September	- Sonny Liston beats Floyd Patterson to become World Heavyweight boxing champion.
October	- 'Love Me Do' the Beatles first single released, but only reaches no 27 in the charts. They also make their first TV appearance.
November	- First edition of 'That Was The Week That Was' seen on BBC TV. Some twelve million viewers eventually tune in for the series.
December	- London brought to a standstill for four days by dense clouds of smog.

No 1 in the music charts at Christmas was 'Return To Sender' by Elvis Presley.

Social Snippet - Was the 1960s the best decade for British TV? In 1962 all these programmes could be seen - 'Come Dancing', 'Panorama', 'The Good Old Days', 'Opportunity Knocks', 'Blue Peter', 'Grandstand', 'Dixon of Dock Green', 'The Saint', 'Juke Box Jury', 'Z Cars', 'Armchair Theatre' and 'The Avengers' (some still running today of course).

Local Film Review: *West Side Story* (shown at the Astoria)

In spite of its artificiality, neo-realism and top-heavy story-line, *West Side Story* is grand entertainment and, for the first two hours of its 151 minutes screen time, is a truly wonderful musical. This is an unusual musical in that its main characters are young hooligans and teenage trollops, there are no lavish settings - most of the action takes place in the slummy streets of New York's West Side, or in sleazy shops and tenement buildings - and the story is quite credible. Although this helps to make *West Side Story* one of the most original musicals ever screened, it also bogs down the picture to some extent. The story becomes so convincing that when the two rival street gangs break into song or leap into a dramatic ballet, the singing and dancing seem artificial and, at the same time, abruptly relegates the story to the background so that it, too, often seems suddenly unreal. And the tragic ending, though entirely logical and necessary to the story-line, has the sobering impact of a bucketful of cold water and leaves one feeling sad and sorry which, though in keeping with the plot, may come as a nasty shock to film fans who go to musicals expecting enchantment and a happy, sunset-tinted finale.

In January 1962 it was announced that the 190 ft chimney of the redundant dust destructor at Hollingdean - seen here - was going to be demolished (work would actually start in May). The destructor building had opened in 1866 on what was then the outskirts of the town, to burn Brighton's rubbish. The chimney was originally 220 ft high, but 30 ft were taken off following a lightning strike in 1952. Incineration stopped that year, with waste going to a site at Sheepcote Valley, off Wilson Avenue, Whitehawk. The Hollingdean site is still used today to house Council cleaning and collecting vehicles, but a plan for a major new incinerator building on the site, now that Sheepcote Valley is full, is a matter of much controversy.

The great local comedian Max Miller opened a new bingo hall at Kemp Town in January 1962, previously the Odeon cinema. This was well known for a bombing incident in September 1940, during World War II, during a matinee show, when fourteen people were killed.

One distinctive vehicle on Brighton's roads in the 1960s was the three or four-wheeled Isetta, better known as the 'Bubble Car'. Local interest here is that for a while, starting in 1957, they'd been manufactured (under licence) in part of the old railway locomotive works located in New England Street, by a firm managed by ex-BOAC pilot, R J Ashley. Ninety cars a week were produced initially. In 1961 BMW took over and moved the production line to Victoria Road, Portslade, where assembly continued until 1964. In a Brighton and Hove Gazette of February 1962, details of these vehicles were given. The price locally was £320/9/- for the standard saloon, £356/1/1 for the Plus model. Both these were of the three-wheel type and gave sixty miles to the gallon. Having only three wheels, a driving licence wasn't needed, only one for a motorcycle. The turning circle required was twenty-five feet and they would fit any garage, the height was only 4ft 4½ ins, the length 7 ft 6ins.

'From the very start,' the report informed readers, 'the Isetta is unconventional. To get in you do not go to the side of it but to the front where the door opens forwards, being hinged on the right. Open it by turning the lever on the right-hand side and it swings outwards, the steering wheel swinging with it to make access easier for the driver. It is easier for the driver to get in first and passengers afterwards, but when getting out the driver should leave last. Controls are fairly conventional, with the clutch pedal on the left of the foot of the steering column, the footbrake pedal, operating hydraulically on all three wheels, on the right of the column and the accelerator pedal on the extreme right.

The report also said that when road-testing the Isetta, 'over poor surfaces the ride is a little harsh.'

Early in 1962, to most people's delight, the Palladium in West Street reverted to its former name of the SS Brighton. February saw the British Toy Fair held in Brighton; a well-known annual event, where toy manufacturers exhibited all their latest products - ready for next Christmas it always seemed!

Seen below, in March, is Max Miller, opening a new betting office for bookmaker Ernest Hayes, in New England Road.

In April, 'a big variety bill' could be seen at the Hippodrome, featuring Dorothy Squires, Tony Osborne and Kenny Baker. This was followed by a production of 'South Pacific', presented by the local Brighton and Hove Operatic Society. The film *The Magnificent Seven* was being screened at the Curzon in Western Road, the Astoria was showing *El Cid*, while *Swiss Family Robinson* was at the Academy in West Street. The Essoldo in North Street was staging a Billy Fury concert.

In April 1962 a ministerial inquiry formally excluded the Grand Hotel from the new development scheme. At the actual West Street/King's Road corner, it was announced that an entertainment centre would be built by the Top Rank group.

'Liberals Give Tories A Shock At Brighton,' ran a Brighton and Hove Gazette headline of May. This was during the local elections when the Liberals finally got its first member onto the town council. Navnit Dholakia defeated reigning Tory councillor Percy Buxton by eighty-seven votes in Pier Ward and left Labour's William Adams 'an also ran'.

In June 1962, following government changes to the gaming laws, Britain's very first legal casino was opened at the Metropole Hotel.

The Queen and the Duke of Edinburgh visited Brighton in July 1962. They had lunch at the Royal Pavilion - 'once again, a reigning monarch and her consort will lunch in the banqueting room' commented the Brighton and Hove Herald, which also pointed out that the builder of the Pavilion, George IV, was the Queen's great-great-great-great-uncle. The couple visited both Brighton College in Eastern Road seen opposite and St Dunstan's, the institute for the blind at Ovingdean. At the college, she was met by its president, Lord Woolton, saw a life-saving demonstration in the swimming pool, watched some cricket practice and a gymnastic display, and then unveiled a plaque outside the chapel. Later, the royal couple went on to Hove to attend a youth rally at the Greyhound Stadium.

Shows to see in Brighton during the summer of 1962 included 'The Wizard of Oz', another ice spectacular at the SS Brighton. The publicity photo here shows one of the cast on 'Supercar', used to transfer Dorothy from Oz back to Kansas at the end of the show. 'Supercar' was, of course, an early Gerry Anderson TV puppet series. At the Hippodrome, 'The Max Bygraves Show' was running, with Benson, Dulay and Company, The Two Tones and the Delrinas. The Palace Pier was again offering plays by its resident repertory company, mainly comedies and Agatha Christie whodunits. There was dancing at the Regent Ballroom as usual. At the Essoldo a mix of films and wrestling could be seen. The Motor Museum attraction, housed in the Aquarium, was charging 2/6 adults, 1/6 children, while to see the sea lions was 2/- adults, 1/- children.

In July 1962, the first commercial water-skiing firm began operating in Brighton. This was run by Gordon Camping (proprietor of the well-known Camping Coaches); 'pick up' would be from the beach between the Palace Pier and East Street, you'd be taken 300 yards out to sea for the skiing. The cost would be 15/- (75p) for fifteen minutes. 'One of the conditions on which the Corporation have insisted is that all skiers wear life jackets.'

A large anti-vivisection campaign was staged in Brighton during July 1962.

Property prices at this time? An advertisement for a flat in the newly built Clivedean Court, off London Road - two bedrooms, lounge, kitchen, bathroom (with use of a private tennis court) was advertised in the local press for £3,195 on a 99-year lease.

August 1962 - a slide down the Palace Pier's helter-skelter gives us a picture that brilliantly personifies the emerging confidence of youth at this time, and its liberation in the years following World War II. Note the 'Teddy Boys' on the left. Teenagers were finding their feet and their voices now, doing more of what they wanted, listening to their own kind of music and going out together without being escorted by adults. As we've seen, coffee bars were springing up to accommodate their socialising, discos their dancing. Soon this assurance would build to almost complete estrangement from adult ways and the 'generation gap' opened up, finding further resolution in extremes of fashion, music and drug taking – aspects of life we now think personify the 1960s. Youngsters were accordingly 'discovered' as a massively exploitable commodity, with a whole array of merchandise aimed increasingly at them, including recorded music, clothing and electrical gadgets.

The teenagers on the helter skelter would almost certainly have seen the machines seen below and others like them, in the Palace of Fun on the pier. Recalling a far more innocent, credulous age, a penny in the slot would bring each tableau to clockwork life; in the Miser's Dream, doors would open, the picture on the wall would slide back, the trunk lid hinge up revealing all sorts of ghosts and horrors, the miser, of course, looking the wrong way each time to

THE MISER'S DREAM

THE HAUNTED HOUSE

see them. Similar horrors would appear with the Haunted House scene. After a minute or so, all disappeared and the scene would resume its original state (unless the clockwork had wound down, then it would have 'frozen' half way through the movement).

There were about a dozen of these mechanical tableaux on the pier, all marvellously made and detailed by specialist maker Nelson Lee, of Blackpool. He operated an amusement arcade there, until retirement, selling the machines off in 1927. Several were bought by a man named Dalton and installed on the Palace Pier, where they survived until 1971. In May 1999, when the pier celebrated its centenary, one of the old machines - The Fortune Teller - was displayed for a while.

Back in August 1960, the local press had reported that the Minister of Transport 'will soon announce his approval' for the parking meter scheme. This duly came through in early September 1962, but he recommended fifty meters should be cut from the scheme.

In the summer of 1962, Lennox Street, off Carlton Hill, was being rebuilt (seen above). There was a scare that the Xaverian College, off Tower Road, north of Queen's Park, would be demolished and a site for a block of flats (it would become a small housing estate in the 1970s) and huge advertisement screens went up in North Street, to mark the start of a large area on the northern side being widened and rebuilt (the properties lost are seen here back in 1961), mostly to alleviate a traffic bottleneck opposite Ship Street.

In September 1962, recording star Frank Ifield ('I Remember You-ooo'), seen on the next page, appeared at the Hippodrome for a week, with ventriloquist Arthur Worsley, Janie Marden and the Kentones. Films were at the Essoldo. At the SS Brighton, pop star Dion Del Shannon appeared (as he called himself then, the Dion was later dropped); wrestling was also on offer.

Jigsaw was a film shot almost entirely in Brighton in 1962. Adapted, produced and directed by Val Guest and starring Jack Warner ('Dixon of Dock Green' TV fame), this was a modest murder mystery based on Hilary Waugh's novel *Sleep Long My Love.*

Some scenes were shot at Lewes, with the key murder taking place at an isolated house - '1 Bungalow Road, Saltdean' - which was fictitious. Brighton scenes included the town's police headquarters (then in Little East Street), an estate agent in Queen's Road, the seafront, Dockerills ironmongers at the corner of Gardner Street and several streets where passing police cars were filmed.

In September the latest plan for the exhibition halls at the rear of the Metropole was unveiled (they seemed to change at this time every week!). The new hall would be 40,000 square feet, four times the size of the town's Corn Exchange building in Church Street, to take any size of trade fair. Harold Poster, seen below, head of AVP (owners of four other hotels in Brighton at this time) said: 'I believe Brighton has the opportunity of becoming the most important town in Europe for these international events, as well

as conferences. Since the Common Market started, such fairs are on the increase. We intend to make a pukka job of it and are considering putting in a sprung floor. It could then be used as a dance hall holding 5000-6000 people and it would have every facility.'

Another massive building project of the 1960s was Sussex University, established on the outskirts of the town, near Falmer village. There had been plans to establish a university in 1911, with £3,000 in funds available, but World War I saw the idea abandoned. Astute Councillor and ex-Mayor Herbert Carden included a university in his ideas for expanding Brighton into 'The City Beautiful' in the 1930s. But it wasn't until June 1958 that the idea finally took off, and with a royal charter granted three years later, the first fifty-two students were accommodated in Preston Road, with lectures taking place at the church hall in Knoyle Road. This would be the first university to open since World War II.

The first building to open at the Sussex University campus, in October 1962, was College House (later renamed Falmer House), the student administrative and recreational building, seen here, plus a three-storey physics block. Designed by Sir Basil Spence, Falmer House is seen here, with a prefab-type building in the far distance on the right, which housed the University's first Barclay's Bank. 'The University is superbly modern and excitingly new', reported the local press. 'Yet, even allowing for the inevitable debris of builders at work, it already has an air of belonging to the beautiful wooden valley in the Downs at Stanmer Park.' These initial buildings were followed by various subject and library areas, the Meeting House opening in October 1966, with Park House, the first of many residential blocks, completed in 1964.

The town also gained a new theatre, built on the university campus, named the Gardner Arts Centre. This was financed by the Gulbenkian Foundation (a Portuguese-based funding body for the arts, established in 1956) and named after its director, Dr. Lytton Gardner. Famed theatre designer Sean Kenny contributed to the design of the building, seen on the next page in 1969. It opened in October that year with a performance of 'Comrade Jacob' by John McGrath.

In October 1962, Little Richard, Dickie Valentine, Tony Hancock and Matt Monroe appeared (in separate shows) at the Hippodrome. These all had a number of supporting acts, and were still the tail end of twice nightly variety in Brighton.

'Brighton children are getting too fat', ran an article in the Brighton and Hove Herald of October 1962 and at Knoll School's speech day, boys in particular were urged to 'develop their brains and their memories'. The first of these strikes a very prescient note, seeing how children's eating habits are big news lately!

In November, more changes to the details of the Metropole's exhibition halls were given. A million pounds would be invested in the development, £50,000 going on air conditioning alone. There would now be two main conference halls - 5000 seats and 2000 seats respectively - which could be linked if needed into one extra large all, making it the biggest exhibition space in the country - at over an acre - except for Earls Court and Olympia. The basement car park would hold 300 cars. The various floors would be linked by escalators (the first in Brighton), with the roof area landscaped as a large garden. Two restaurants, bars and a quick-service counter would also be provided. The highest block of flats in Sussex would be part of the scheme, 250 ft in height.

There was only one really seasonal show in Brighton over the Christmas period of 1962-63; the pantomime 'Robin Hood', starring Roy Castle, at the Hippodrome. 'The whole story is a cheery, happy Christmas panto', reported the local press, 'notable for its very high standards of music, dancing and production, and very welcome for the complete absence of questionable jokes'.

The Regent cinema showed the old Bing Crosby movie, *White Christmas*. Oddly, two Shakespearian plays - 'Julius Caesar' and 'The Tempest', fully staged by the Old Vic company, could be seen at the Essoldo in December, and the strange mixture of films and live events playing this venue shows how the management were grasping at any straw to keep it open.

There was no ice show at the SS Brighton and in the very last Brighton and Hove Herald of 1962 came the bombshell news that it was to be demolished as part of the final plan for the King's Road/West Street corner. However, the Rank organisation assured everyone their new Top Rank Centre would have a new 'upstairs' skating rink where ice hockey would continue. Covered over, this would double as a conference hall capable of seating 6000 people. There would be a luxury underground cinema, a ballroom, a thirty-two lane ten-pin bowling centre with licensed club, a banqueting hall, a hotel with rooftop restaurant, plus an arcade of shops and a continental-style café.

1963

Some Key Events:

January	- Charles De Gaulle vetoes UK entry into EEC.
February	- 'Please Please Me' the Beatles' second single reaches no 2 in the charts.
March	- Alcatraz, the US penitentiary, closes and the last twenty-seven prisoners transferred.
May	- 'From Me To You' the Beatles third single reaches no 1 in the charts.
June	- John Profumo, Minister of War in the Macmillan government, resigns over 'impropriety' with showgirl Christine Keeler - the so-called 'Profumo Affair'.
July	- The Rolling Stones make their first TV appearance on 'Thank Your Luck Stars'.
August	- The Great Train Robbery - armed robbers stop the Glasgow to London train at Sears Crossing, Buckinghamshire, and haul over £2 million.
September	- Christine Keeler arrested for perjury; she later receives a nine-month prison sentence. The Denning report into the Profumo affair is also published.
November	- President John F Kennedy assassinated in Dallas, Texas.
December	- Birth of future movie star Brad Pitt.

No 1 in the music charts at Christmas was 'I Want To Hold Your Hand' by the Beatles.

Social snippet - The so-called 'Cold War' and the build up of nuclear weapons by Russia and the USA caused huge concern in the West and the 'Bay of Pigs' episode, of 1961, where it looked as if a shooting match might actually start, was a key incident. In April 1963, 70,000 marched from Aldermaston to London to demonstrate against the manufacture and stockpiling of nuclear weapons.

Local Film Review: *The Birds* (shown at the Odeon)
'I have seen *The Birds* this week... it's the most genuinely frightening film that I have ever seen. It builds up into a magnificent and violent climax that had me stuck in my seat with half my finger-nails bitten off.'

'The week of heroes; the week when postmen, milkmen, coalmen, even the dustmen, took on the stature of giants; the week when ordinary men and women battled through arctic conditions to get to work; the week when Brighton suburbs learnt what it meant to be cut off from the outside world.' This was how the Brighton and Hove Herald reported the heavy snow that fell in Brighton over the Christmas and New Year period (it would carry on, intermittently, until March); there was skiing in Preston Park and a full-sized igloo appeared in the playground of Hangleton Junior School. Sporting events were badly hit, but many could watch the Brighton Tiger's first ever Saturday afternoon match, against their main south-coast rivals, the Southampton Vikings, televised live by the BBC on 'Grandstand'. Later, power cuts added to the misery of the big freeze and at one point, Christmas tree candles were used to light wards in the Royal Sussex County Hospital. An elderly woman in an oxygen tent in Bevendean Hospital was only saved by emergency power relayed from an ice-cream van. The photograph here shows snow falling in North Street the following month.

A press item of January 1963 on the price of houses in Brighton stated: 'There has been a heavy demand for the average, semi-detached three-bedroomed house between £3,500 and £4,500 and it has been almost impossible to satisfy the demand.' The price for a luxury bungalow at this time was about £15,000!

In January came the news that Sir Keith Joseph, Minister of Housing and Local Government, had passed the scheme for the West Street site (which would become the Churchill Square development), after a public inquiry lasting nine months. However, as we've seen, he did not allow the compulsory purchase order on the Grand Hotel, which was to have been demolished and replaced by an amusement centre, nor did he allow the building of a new hotel on the corner of West Street, where he recommended building 'a place of assembly'. Joseph stated, 'to build an amusement centre on the site of the Grand Hotel would be harmful to the surroundings and that the site chosen for the new hotel to be built in replacement is unsuitable for the purpose'. Other than these provisos, the scheme could go ahead.

A roundup of entertainment in January saw Sir Adrian Boult conducting an orchestral concert at the Dome, the Essoldo featured the Royal Ballet, the Regent was showing *The Longest Day*, the Theatre Royal had a revue starring Michael Flanders and Donald Swan, entitled, 'At The Drop Of A Hat', and at the neighbouring Paris Cinema, *Passionate Dreams* was shown as a double bill with *The Young Have No Morals*. These would be among the last films it was to show. And at the Hippodrome it was announced that after the 'Robin Hood' pantomime finished in early February, the theatre would close for five weeks. Moss Empires', its owners, said: 'There is no question that the theatre is closing down'.

In January, while the annual British Toy Fair was being held at several venues, including the SS Brighton, a row broke out between what were now seen as rival plans for trade and conference facilities in Brighton. Harold Poster, commenting on Rank's plans for the West Street site, said: 'Brighton needs one large conference hall – but only one. At present we are suffering from starvation in conference halls but if we get two it will be indigestion'.

January was when New England House, off London Road, opened (seen opposite). This was another high-rise block, but to house light industry, and was seen as 'Brighton's answer to the problem of accommodation for local industries displaced by compulsory purchase orders or for those in zones designated under the town's development plan'. The Dolphin Press was the first firm to move in.

January also saw the huge George Hotel being demolished at the bottom of West Street in readiness for the new Top Rank building. This is in the centre, left, and would complete the full widening of West Street, which started opposite the Clock Tower, back in the 1920s!

Two illuminations were proposed at this time, to brighten up the seafront. Everyone remembers them - the 'rotosphere' (most people called it 'the sputnik') and a peacock. The cost would be £2,700.

Early in February came a statement from the Corporation that the cost of snow clearance to date had been £42,000. It was also reported by the organisers of the Toy Fair that trade had been hit because of the new parking meters. The final design for the Top Rank building was revealed in February too - the all-too familiar low, box building that was subsequently built, with the spiky, gold, 'crenellated' roofline.

Gerry and the Pacemakers appeared at the Hippodrome in February, so did John Leyton ('Johnny Remember Me') with the Rolling Stones - seen opposite.

Standing in New Road, just a few doors down from the Theatre Royal, the Paris Cinema was for most of its hundred-years of life, a music hall and variety theatre; it closed in March 1963. It had an amazing history and *nine* different names over the years. It began life in the summer of 1863, as the Pavilion Wine and Spirit Music Rooms, but within months had become the Oxford Theatre of Varieties. Over the years it was home to such music hall greats as Dan Leno, George Robey, Little Titch, Marie Lloyd, Tom Costello and Albert Chevalier. Rebuilding after a fire of March 1867 saw the first change of name, to the New Oxford. Over the next ten decades, it became the Empire, Coliseum, Court, Dolphin, Her Majesties and finally the Paris. The appeal of early cinema saw the theatre showing films from 1909 and the building was subsequently bought by Gaumont British as one of their chain of 150 cinemas. Between 1947 and 1955 it was a theatre again, converting a final time to the Paris Cinema. Playwright J.B. Priestley called the building, 'the loveliest theatre I have seen on the South Coast.'

A small story that had a big impact came in March 1963 when it was announced that 'Kim', Brighton's only resident police horse, was going to be 'sacked' at a saving of 30/- a week. The Watch Committee had been told - as had all the other Council committees - to try to cut 2% from their estimated budgets for the next financial year, so it recommended that eleven-year-old Kim be sold. It was thought to be one of the few economies the Watch Committee could actually make, as most of the money they spent was on police wages over which they had no control. Kim actually cost about £13 a week to keep, half met by a Government grant. A fine bay gelding, he was bought from the Metropolitan Police Riding School in July 1960, following duty at the wedding of Princess Margaret. During the summer months he was usually on patrol

on the seafront and a popular sight.

March also was the month when details were given of a £250,000 development scheme for the Lanes, to be known as Brighton Square; work in progress is seen opposite. Hanningtons, the large department store owned the 2$\frac{1}{2}$ acre site in partnership with the Church Commissioners of England and the plan was to form an attractive square that would connect with the Lanes and Brighton Place. Below ground level would be a large garage, above would be twenty-four shops grouped round the square and along the linking passageways. Above the shops would be fifteen maisonettes and flats. The main site of the square was unknown to the public - it was privately owned - and mainly occupied by sheds, workshops and garages, plus several old overgrown gardens. The architects would be Fitzroy Robinson and Partners. 'A start will be made immediately' announced the local press, 'and it is expected that the development will be completed and ready for occupation by December 1964.'

Entertainment on offer in Brighton during March and April continued to see the demise of variety and the pop concert take over. Frank Ifield, Brenda Lee and Cliff Richard and the Shadows - seen above - could all be seen at the Hippodrome. The Red Army singers, dancers and musicians also appeared and two musicals were staged - 'Gentlemen Prefer Blondes' and 'Stop The World I Want To Get Off'. At the Dome, Ella Fitzgerald and Oscar Peterson were featured in concert, and later Shirley Bassey and Matt Monroe appeared together, accompanied by John Barry's Orchestra. The Essoldo struggled on with X films.

But the entertainment world remembers 1963 as the year comic legend Max Miller died. He's pictured opposite in April, at his Kemp Town home, 25 Burlington Street, where he'd lived since 1948. His real name was Thomas Sargent and he was, without doubt, the best stand-up comedian of his generation. Like the town's seaside rock, he was Brighton through and through; his 'naughty but nice' material echoed vulgar, seaside postcards of the 'where's my little Willie?' variety and completely at one with Brighton's racy image.

Born in Hove, he'd begun his professional career in 1919, with a concert party group that performed on the seafront and West Pier run by Jack Sheppard. He went on to appear as principal comedian in Tom Arnold's show, 'Piccadilly', in 1926 and in time became one of the highest paid performers in the business, appearing in three Royal Variety shows (1931, 1937 and 1950) and making a number of films.

Miller's last stage appearance was in December 1960. In May 1963, at the age of 69, he died - a local hero. His home theatre, the Hippodrome, where he had performed so often, particularly during World War II, 'died' too - closing just a year later, becoming a bingo hall. A statue of Miller now stands in New Road, unveiled in May 2005 by Sir Norman Wisdom.

Another major personality to die in 1963 [1960] was Gilbert Harding who was probably the most well-known resident of Brighton in the late 1950s, due to frequent TV appearances. Born in a Midland's workhouse where his father presided, he went to Cambridge University, but subsequently took ordinary jobs as a teacher and policeman. He emigrated to Canada, but returned to Britain to do broadcasting work at the BBC during the war.

The radio show, 'Twenty Questions', saw Harding's rise to fame, increasing with the famous early TV show, 'What's My Line?' People tuned in just to see Harding and the mood he was in. He could be utterly charming or downright rude by turns, and occasionally appeared drunk. At the Theatre Royal in Brighton, he would often call things out in the middle of a performance, if he didn't think the play or actors were up to it and people would go to the Royal hoping to hear him heckle.

Harding always stood up for ordinary people though, supported charities and startled everyone when he broke down and cried during a famous TV interview with John Freeman on the programme, 'Face To Face'. Drinking, smoking and ill health took their toll and he died, aged only fifty-two, on the steps of Broadcasting House, London.

May saw Bruce Forsyth appear at the Hippodrome and later the same month, the legendary Sammy Davis Junior appeared for two nights. Del Shannon appeared again at the Essoldo. In June, the Palace Pier Repertory Company started up again, with plays such as 'Private Lives'. The big ice show, at the SS Brighton for the summer of 1963, would be 'Peter Pan', starting in July. 'Tom Arnold has done it again, bless him', wrote the Brighton and Hove Herald, reviewing the show. 'He's given Brighton a knockout show in Peter Pan at the Sports Stadium. It's a dazzler in the spectacular tradition.' As it turned out, this would be the last ever ice show at the SS Brighton.

Throughout the 1960s, six girls known as the Promettes could be found at various locations around the town, acting as weekend tourist guides. This idea had started up in the 1950s and they were a regular feature of Brighton's summer season. The girls for the 1963 season are seen on the next page by the side of the outdoor bathing pool at Black Rock. They could usually speak several languages between them and in their famous shoulder bags were all kinds of timetables and lists, so that any query posed by lost tourists could be answered. They were used for all kinds of publicity stunts too, once famously taking turkeys on leads along the seafront, to promote a campaign by

the British Turkey Federation. Their base was a caravan parked on the seafront between the piers. Their pay? Expenses only it seems!

A plan for the paddle steamer 'Consul' to operate trips between the Palace Pier and Eastbourne emerged in July 1963. Coming over from its berth in Newhaven, it would leave the pier twice a week at 10 am and return at 6.30.

July saw a popular 'sporting' event take place on Madeira Drive, which is now just a memory. This was the National Scouter Car Races, nicknamed the 'Soap Box Derby', which had started way back in 1939. As the name implies, this was for scouting groups to build go-carts and enter them for races. There were three categories of entry - novice, premiere and open, the last being for more elaborate or 'off-beat' entries. One rule was that only £8 in total was allowed to be spent on each cart. Entries in 1963 came from as far afield as Leamington Spa, Purley and Bournemouth. The event was presided over by Mayor, Councillor Stanley Deason, with prizes presented by variety star Dickie Henderson - seen below.

Henderson was appearing in the summer show at the Hippodrome, *Light Up The Town* along with Eve Boswell and the Tiller Girls. A feature of this show was a spectacular waterfall scene, set on a tropical island. The big film at the Regent was *Lawrence of Arabia*. The Essoldo was showing X-certificate films again and also staging wrestling.

Some lettered badges being sold from shops on the lower promenade between the piers caused a stir in the summer of 1963. 'I am a psychiatrist, lie down' was one of them. The other had 'I am a Virgin Islander.' These had been banned at Southend and there were complaints in Brighton they were offensive. At 2/11 each, one trader said,' they sell very well, particularly at weekends.'

July (a busy month!) also saw plans for the town's very first multi-storey car park unveiled. This was on the site of the old Grand Theatre, at the top of North Road, which burnt down in 1961. The site was actually owned by impresario Tom Arnold, producer of the ice shows at the SS Brighton. 200 cars would be accommodated.

Clearance for the Churchill Square site was taking place at this time. As already said, one significant street partially lost in 1963 was Grenville Place, immediately south of Western Road, at its North Street end. It was one of the first streets to be built in the whole area, even before Western Road existed, the earliest

record of it being in 1803, when a weather report states that houses under construction in the street were damaged by storms. It seems to have been completely built up by the 1820s. The southern side, seen opposite, which contained some really delightful, cobble-faced houses with bow windows, came down first - in 1963 - but the northern side survived for another four years. 'It was one of those attractive small streets that have helped to give Brighton so much character', wrote Antony Dale, in 1976. As we've seen, parking meters, seen here on the northern side, appeared in Brighton during the spring of 1963 and caused all sorts of ructions and complaints about them seemed unending. They were eventually removed in favour of a voucher system, early in 1991.

At the Albion Hill site, a school at the end of Claremont Row (below), one of the last large buildings in the whole redevelopment area, was about to come down. Originally Richmond Street School, dating from 1873, it later amalgamated with Sussex Street School, which stood at the other end of the street. The whole of the western side of Claremont Row was occupied by these two school buildings with playgrounds in between. Classes were often very large. An inspector's report of 1930 showed that several had over fifty pupils in them! The premises were last used as an infant school and the ground floor for meetings of the local Nautical Training Corps, but closed in 1962 and demolished during the following year.

In August 1963, the celebrated missionary Gladys Aylward gave a talk at the Dome on her life and work. She'd also recently been the subject for a 'This Is Your Life' programme on TV.

The paddle steamer Consul's short season took place as planned, ending in early August. This is almost certainly the last time a paddle steamer ever worked a season of excursions from either pier at Brighton.

During the same month, another old mode of transport, Volk's Railway, which began running in 1883, celebrated eighty years of service. When it first ran, the Daily Telegraph commented: 'Volk's Electric Railway, which has been constructed on the upper part of the beach along Madeira Road, is a very interesting practical application of electricity. A large number of passengers are continually amusing themselves with this means of transit. In the warm weather visitors will be glad to avail themselves of it to reach the extreme end of the town, a rather fatiguing walk up the cliff. The young people are delighted with the novelty.' All this still seemed to apply in 1963 and still applies today.

August saw a plea for more girls to enter the annual 'Miss Brighton' contest. 'In an effort to increase the number of entries,' the organisers announced, 'the winner this year will receive a cash prize of £20, in addition to representing Brighton in the 'Miss Southern Belle' TV contest organised by Southern TV. She will also be provided with a swimsuit of her choice, a pair of shoes and a free hairstyle for her appearance in the television programme, which will be transmitted on the evening of Wednesday October 30th.' The winner – out of thirteen entrants - would turn out to be Jackie Peterson who had won 'Miss Brighton' two years previously. The judges, led by Dickie Henderson, gave her almost maximum marks for personality, speech and appearance, it was reported.

In August 1963, the foundation stone was laid for a new Brighton church. This was the £40,000 Ebenezer Strict Baptist Chapel, on the corner of Ivory Place, which would replace an older chapel, in Richmond Street, seen here, compulsorily acquired by the Corporation as part of the Albion Hill scheme. This had opened in 1825 and was affectionately known by youngsters in the area as the 'Lemon Squeezer'. It came down in 1966 and the new church opened in 1965, designed by C J Wood.

'NEW CHAPEL FOR OLD'

AN architect's drawing of the £40,000 new Ebenezer Strict Baptist Chapel which is to replace the present building in Richmond-street, compulsorily acquired by Brighton Corporation.

The stone-laying ceremony is to be performed by Pastor James Payne on Saturday next, August 10, at 3.30 p.m., and it is hoped that the new chapel will be completed in about a year.

Members are pleased with the Corporation's "new chapel for old" offer. "The Corporation have co-operated with us wonderfully well," said Pastor Payne. "The new building will be on the corner of Ivory-place, a little lower down the hill, and this will be welcomed by the old people who find it difficult to get to our chapel at the moment."

Entertainment in September 1963 saw another mixed bag. There was ice skating and wrestling at the SS Brighton, *Lawrence of Arabia* was still at the Regent, Hitchcock's *The Birds* was at the Academy (earlier it had been the Odeon) and X-rated films were being shown at the Essoldo. The Essoldo reverted to pop later in the month, with two shows featuring top stars Billy Fury, Joe Brown and the Bruvvers, The Tornadoes and Marty Wilde. The Theatre Royal saw a visit from the Fol-de-Rols company, which presented old-style variety shows and, on the Palace Pier, the annual repertory season ended with Agatha Christie's, 'Peril at End House'.

In September 1963 came what seemed to be the final details of the Western Road/seafront plan. It was back to eleven acres in size and still take five years to build at a cost of £8 million. The shopping area (not named Churchill Square yet) would consist of eighty-four shops, two department stores, a supermarket, restaurant, petrol station and two public houses. There would be 80,000 square feet of office space and over thirty flats. 1905 car parking spaces would be provided, 1000 for public use. The Top Rank Centre would contain a ballroom, a two-level bowling alley (sixteen lanes each), an ice rink, restaurant, a conference hall to hold 4000 people, plus fourteen shops.

In October 1963, a black Cadillac pulled up outside the Royal Pavilion and a young Arab gentleman stepped out, wearing flowing robes and headdress, accompanied by a private secretary and travel aide. This was Prince Emir Khalid ibn Abdul Asir ibn Saud, fourth son of King Saud of Arabia, who was respectfully greeted by the Pavilion's Director, Clifford Musgrave, and then given a guided tour of the building as was usual with all dignitaries visiting Brighton wishing to see the Pavilion. Tea followed in the Committee Room. Suitably impressed and pleased with the cordiality of his reception, the Prince made his farewells, returned to his Cadillac and was driven away. Nothing seemed amiss - just another VIP making a visit - until local papers appeared later in the day exposing the whole thing as a hoax. 'Paddy's Prank' (as it became known) had been thought up by a nineteen-year-old building student, Patrick Cook, from Brighton College of Technology. He'd spent three months in the Middle East studying architecture and had obtained his robe and headdress there. His knowledge of Arabic was good enough to reply to an off the cuff remark made by one of the Pavilion's attendants. Later, Musgrave and the others present at the visit said they knew it was a hoax but went along with it, as it would have been, 'a pity to spoil the perpetrators' fun when they had gone to such great trouble, and the history of the Royal Pavilion would not have been complete without an event like this once in a while'.

Leslie Kramer, a Brighton entertainments promoter, planned a number of new attractions at Devil's Dyke during the early 1960s, estimated to cost a quarter of a million pounds. These included a full-sized replica of a Sussex windmill near the hotel and, amazingly, a one-fifth replica of Egypt's temple of Abu Simbel, which would have been built into the side on the gorge. These plans, which were later modified, included a pet's corner, a show-jumping arena, model village and sea-lion pool, came before the Corporation in October 1963 and only failed by one vote to get passed. Mr Kramer persevered though and in the spring of 1964 managed to get the pet's corner attraction open at the Dyke.

In the autumn came an announcement of another plan that would change Brighton forever. 'A £9 million scheme for a yachting marina at Brighton, which would be situated east of the Palace Pier and be unique in the world, is going before Brighton Planning Committee,' announced the Brighton and Hove Herald in October 1963. 'Put forward by private developers,' it continued, 'the scheme includes a helicopter port among many other amenities. Harbour walls would be built out to sea providing facilities inside for yachting under ideal conditions. Around would be floating anchorages and slipways. Tiers of flatlets will overlook the marina, which will also include in one huge self-contained unit, a hotel, shops, club houses, swimming pool etc. A casino, too, is proposed so that the Marina would capture the gay atmosphere of the French and Italian Riviera. Buildings would be well below the height of Marine Parade thereby preventing any interference with views over the Marina and out to sea. Ranking among the most ambitious schemes that have yet been proposed, it would make Brighton a yachting centre of international importance.'

The Planning Committee's approval for the scheme was probably the easiest part of the project to achieve. Ahead lay many years of chequered progress before work would actually start on the project in the 1970s.

In November, the new Eagle Star insurance building opened in Queen's Road. This was on the site of Churchill House, seen on page 16, previously an old dispensary building.

LANDSCAPE DESIGN FOR PROPOSED UNDERGROUND CAR PARK AT REGENCY SQUARE, BRIGHTON, 1 for the BRIGHTON CORPORATION DESIGN SUBMITTED BY:

Plans for a very controversial underground car park under Regency Square (seen here) came before the Council in November and were approved (and later built).

Billy J Kramer and the Dakotas appeared at the Hippodrome in November and the Christmas pantomime for 1963 there would be 'The Frog Prince'. The cast included Charlie Cairoli, Freddie Frinton and Billy Dainty. One unusual aspect of this production was a scene where the princess threw a ball down the well for the frog to fetch. A screen was lowered and a short piece of animated film was run, showing the frog down the well and some of the creatures he encountered; one was an octopus! However, as it turned out, this would be the old theatre's very last pantomime.

The Eagle Star
Insurance
building in
Queens Road,
opened in
November 1963.

1964

Some Key Events:

March	- Radio Caroline begins broadcasting from a ship ten miles off the Suffolk coast - one of the early so-called 'pirate' radio stations. Within two months it had seven million listeners.
April	- TV sees a new channel start - BBC 2.
May	- The first Habitat store opens in London's Fulham Road.
June	- Nelson Mandela and seven others sent to prison in South Africa (Robben Island prison).
July	- Total deaths - to date - of US soldiers involved in the Vietnam War given as 399.
September	- The Daily Herald newspaper ceases publication and is replaced by The Sun.
October	- Martin Luther King receives Nobel Peace Prize (its youngest ever recipient). 15th Olympic Games held in Tokyo, Japan. Four Gold medals won by Britain.
November	- The death penalty is abolished in the UK.

No 1 in the music charts at Christmas was 'I Feel Fine' by The Beatles.

Social Snippet - In a 1964 UK survey, 16% of youngsters between the ages of fifteen and nineteen said they'd had some kind of sexual experience. Ten years later, this figure had virtually doubled.

Local Film Review; *Goldfinger* (shown at the Odeon)

Goldfinger is bigger and better than its two predecessors, and is a brilliant example of the commercial cinema at its best. Status symbols, gadgets and psuedo-science abound. There's Bond's car for instance, an Aston Martin DB5 with smoke and oil-slick sprays at the rear, bullet-proof windows, machine guns hidden in the front headlights and an ejector seat for unwelcome passengers. As ever he is surrounded by a harem of girls. Shirley Eaton's gilt-edged death is one of the kinkiest moments in the film. Gert Frobe makes a magnificent Goldfinger and Sean Connery is more impeccable, even wittier and far more dangerous-looking than ever before as 007.

News of a very substantial rehousing scheme - to last seven years - was in the news during January 1964. In its way this was almost the Kemp Town equivalent of the Albion Hill Redevelopment Scheme. A joint meeting of the Town Planning and Housing Committees agreed that a substantial number of streets in Kemp Town would be demolished and the displaced tenants rehoused in new property in the same area. The streets involved were Essex Street, Hereford Street, St Mary's Place, Warwick Street, Lavender Street (seen above left), Montague Street and Place, Upper Bedford Street, plus parts of Eastern Road and Upper St James' Street. 'Already', it was stated, 'two thirteen-storey blocks of flats are climbing skywards (above) and will probably be ready for occupation at the end of next summer.' Shops in Upper St James' Street would be the last to go (probably, it was thought, in 1971) and by then twice as many people would be accommodated in the area than at the start of the scheme. All this came about, again redrawing the map of Brighton, this time between Eastern Road and Upper St James' Street.

In February 1964, an ancient - and really unique - circular stone tank, twelve feet across - seen here - was suddenly discovered in the basement of a bookshop in the Lanes. The Lanes area was once called the Hempshares, a site where hemp was grown to make rope for the town's fishermen. The tank was thought to be a 'soak' for hemp, to soften up the fibres, so they could be teased out and made up into different types of cords and ropes.

Also in February 1964 the Argus had an interesting article about Brighton's pubs. With the Albion Hill Redevelopment Scheme really up and running now, many 'locals' in the area were closing, as were its beer houses - 'once a second home to the working classes' - which were pubs that only sold beer, not spirits, a real relic of Brighton's back street life. In fact there were 311 fully licensed public houses in Brighton at this time, with only eleven beer houses left. Only nine years previously, in 1953, there had been 288 pubs and sixty-seven beer houses.

The London Arms, in Lennox Street (seen on the next page), part of the redevelopment site, was one of these beer shops about to close. A compulsory purchase order had been on it for three years, so it was really on borrowed time. Mrs Rose Stevens, the licensee's wife commented: 'Everyone says this is the best little pub round here. I know you can't get spirits, but you can always nip across the road for one. These posh pubs today - the working classes don't like them. They prefer the old beer houses every time.'

Ted Purdin, despite being licensee of the County Oak, Hollingbury, one of Brighton's newest and smartest pubs, said: 'A lot of people feel uncomfortable in a spacious pub. They would rather have the old dartboard and old wooden chairs than the plush carpets and cocktail bar which are being featured today. A lot of the old people like the beer houses because there is more atmosphere in them. They have been brought up in them. But once you grant a beer house a full licence, then the whole atmosphere seems to change. Alterations are made and the regulars don't like it. They would rather have their

old, smoky taproom any day. And I must say that, nowadays, people drink 'shorts' just for the snob value. This has partly contributed to the downfall of the old beer house.' Similar sorts of things would be said in the 1990s, when traditional style pubs became 'theme pubs', taking on absurd, new names, pumping out loud music and appealing to a younger clientele!

In March 1964, right out of the blue, news came that plans for a massive tower, to stand between the piers on the seafront, were seriously being considered by the town's planning committee. Costing £1 million, it was to be known as 'The Skydeck'. 'Gleaming like a silver rocket by day,' stated the Brighton Herald, 'aglow from the restaurant decking at night, and outrageously modern, it will attract thousands just for the chance to see the unrivalled view from the observation decking 600ft over the sea.'

The tower itself was to be 1000ft high, built at the end of a 300ft pier.

There would be three decks to the pier, for bars, a restaurant and a marine-type attraction where 'larger fish, such as dolphins and porpoises could be watched.' Three lifts, travelling 700ft a minute would carry 1,500 people an hour to the observation deck.

The proposers stated, 'The Eiffel Tower in Paris is seventy-five years old, yet last year it had a record number of visitors. In New York, the observation platforms at the top of such buildings as the Empire State are a major tourist attraction. We have studied towers all over the world and they fascinate people.'

This extraordinary proposal obviously came to nothing - it was just too extreme a structure for the town's seafront - even in the 1960s - but is a good example of '1960s might-have-been Brighton'.

The following month, Brighton's original Bedford Hotel, near the West Pier, caught fire. Hundreds of Easter-week visitors packed the seafront to watch, with a police cordon forming in case any of the building came crashing down. Two people died in the blaze.

Although only the roof and upper storeys were destroyed (seen below) the whole building was later demolished. Strangely, proposals to pull the hotel down and replace it with a larger, modern building had gone before the Council only a matter of weeks before the fire. Councillor Lewis Cohen stated: 'This is a hotel which is completely out of date. The people who are proposing to rebuild the Bedford are doing a marvellous job of work for Brighton.'

The hotel was designed by Thomas Cooper (he also planned Brighton's 1830-31 Town Hall) opening in October 1829. Charles Dickens wrote much of *Dombey and Son* while staying at the building. When the Royal Pavilion had been vacated and sold to the town in 1850, royal visitors customarily stayed at the Bedford.

The new hotel would open in September 1967 (presently called the Holiday Inn), and was the first significant new hotel in the town for fifty years. Its design though was very 'state-of-the-art' and it's changed name several times since; at present (2006) it's the Holiday Inn. Anthony Seldon, in *Brave New City* says, 'it will be hard to find a starker contrast anywhere of the beautiful being replaced by the gross. In every sense, a disgrace.'

At the top of the next page left, another picture where youth predominates. This is the scene on Dalton's Beach, the one immediately east of the Palace Pier, which appears to be taken over by teenagers. The date is the Bank Holiday of April 1964. Not long after this picture was taken, the infamous deck-chair fight between Mods and Rockers took place on the Aquarium terraces. This huge group all seem to be Mods, judging from their dress and as every one seems calm and relaxed, the picture was probably taken shortly before the Rockers arrived. The view below it seems to show an early arrest.

Above is probably the most compelling and well-known image of the entire post-war period in Brighton. Mods are trying to drive Rockers from the terrace under a salvo of deck chairs, some having to drop over the balustrade, onto Madeira Drive, the fight is now thought to have been staged for a member of the press (rumours that a ten-shilling note exchanged hands) who wasn't prepared to wait around until something spontaneous happened. If you look, those seemingly being attacked by the Mods just look like more Mods. Whatever the situation, there were some fifty arrests and twenty-six youths came before the courts the following day. Two were sentenced to three months imprisonment and nine others went to a detention centre for the same period. The fighting was considered the worst outbreak of teenage violence the country had ever seen and the local press referred to it as the 'Battle of Brighton.' In the Daily Mirror Marje Proops wrote: ' It is a pity, in a way, we can't just hand over a few old deckchairs and a deserted chunk of Brighton Beach and seal it all off and let them

play their ridiculous kids's games so we could snooze in the sun in peace. But they wouldn't care for that.'

The view opposite was taken during the early evening of the Bank Holiday Monday, when things had calmed down somewhat.

In later years a ploy of the police to prevent similar incidents in the town was to confiscate Mods' scooters and Rockers' bikes and take them to Devil's Dyke, where they could be recovered, but only after a huge walk to get there!

The rise of various youth cultures since World War II was itself a startling development, and the 1960s now seems the formative decade for this. The Mod ideal centred on stylish clothing, pop music, dancing and the all-important motor scooter, which symbolised liberty from adult parameters. In the precision of dress, they were really the successors of Teddy Boys from the 1950s. Rockers liked heavy rock music and wore studded leather gear, chains and black ex-Air Force boots. They rode powerful motorbikes trying to reach 100 m.p.h. ('doing the ton') whenever they could get away with it.

Rockers considered Mods to be puny, effeminate, even homosexual, so saw them as fair game for a bashing and the two groups, with their vastly differing outlooks, became enemy factions during the decade, resulting in many clashes, particularly at seaside resorts. With other disturbances in places like Bournemouth and Margate in 1964, questions about teenage violence were raised in Parliament, there was talk of vigilantes being formed to deal with any further trouble, and calls for the cat-o-nine tails to be used on convicted offenders.

Other groups would emerge later, such as the flower-power 'children' who wanted to 'make love not war' and Brighton - of course - saw its fair share of them too.

In May 1964, the Essoldo finally threw in the towel and closed as a theatre and cinema, becoming a full-time bingo hall. Despite trying anything and everything to keep going, it had struggled on and lost out, mostly to the Hippodrome, also to the Regent cinema (just round the corner in Queen's Road) and also of course, from the impact of TV. As we've seen, it really had tried everything to keep going though.

'Survey Shows Students Are Conservative, Decent' ran the headline of a Brighton and Hove Herald of July 1964. The survey was carried out on students at Brighton Technical College - 300 questionnaires were distributed - the sixty questions were mostly about politics, sex and religion - and surprised the organisers as responses were far less radical than expected. Seventy-three percent said they were

Christians, thirty-nine percent supported the Conservative party, fourteen percent the socialists, with sixty-eight percent against divorce. Sixty-three percent were against 'free love', ninety percent considered coloured people weren't inferior to whites and fifty-four percent were in favour of flogging for sex crimes. They were also asked for their opinion on Jews for some reason. Sixty-seven percent answered 'they are as valuable as any one else.' Sixty-seven percent were also against blood sports and sixty percent thought war was 'inherent in human nature.'

'One thing that this report proves conclusively,' said Andre Hare, a member of the student council and co-organiser of the survey, 'is the students at the college, if nowhere else, are, on the whole decent, sane-minded and clean-living young people.'

In July, the Duke of Richmond and Gordon, president of the Sussex Association of Boy's Clubs, laid the foundation stone of new premises for Brighton Boy's Club in Edward Street. The previous building had gone due to the road-widening scheme taking place at this time, seen above. 'What the Boys' Club stands for is almost a national emergency,' said the Duke. 'This club shows that things really can be done if people are determined.'

The picture opposite shows the ceremony, with the club's Chaplain, the Reverend Peter Campbell, Vicar of St John's Church, Carlton Hill, blessing the building. The new club would have games' rooms, workshops and a special roof playground, as well as general offices and a caretaker's flat. The club's previous premises were opened in 1927 (by the Prince of Wales) in a building that was once an old cinema (the Tierney) at a cost of just £5000.

Two youths, one aged twenty, the other aged seventeen, came before magistrates following 'an orgy of destruction' in July 1964. They had stolen two cars and property inside them, damaged another car by throwing bricks at it and also stolen some tools from a further vehicle. They had no insurance cover either. Twenty-two further offences were taken into consideration. The seventeen-year-old fainted during the proceedings. The Recorder was Mr J A Doughty QC, MP, who sentenced them to 'a period of Borstal training.'

The enormous vending machine seen opposite, known as the Automat, opened at the top of North Street, near the Clock Tower, in July 1964. It offered a choice of more that 200 items, from hot meals, such as a plate of eggs and bacon, sixteen varieties of sandwiches, or even a pair of stockings 'as a replacement for the pair that ladder on a way to a date.' This was the first machine of its kind in the southeast, although there were one or two operating in London; it caused quite a stir.

Singer Ray Charles appeared at the Dome, in July, but this month in Brighton 1964 is remembered for Beatlemania taking the town by storm. 'The Beatles Show' (as it was quaintly called) came to the Hippodrome, with a ticket in the stalls costing 15/- (75p today). Stories about the two concerts they gave (the second was in October) are legendary. Most of those present say they couldn't hear what was being sung at all due to the screaming girl fans and

when the sound system packed up for a short period, no-one noticed because of the din. In fact no one interviewed about the concert can recall a specific song at all, such was the row. Getting the Beatles into the Hippodrome without being mobbed, caused some managerial head scratching, until someone decided to utilise a garage building standing immediately opposite the theatre (today a housing development). Middle Street was closed off and the van containing the Fab Four drove down West Street, which no one was expecting, then into the garage, which had a West Street entrance. The group dashed through to Middle Street and ran across the street, through the Hippodrome's front doors, with the crowds getting all but a fleeting glimpse of them as they passed.

All of this is borne out by the review of the show that appeared in the Brighton and Hove Herald, given in full here -

THIS IS BEATLEMANIA! Four Lonely Young Men and Screams - Screams - Screams

---

BRIGHTON HIPPODROME

ARTHUR HOWES and BRIAN EPSTEIN present

THE BEATLES

1st Performance 6-0

SUNDAY
JULY 12

STALLS
15/-

J25 CENTRE

TO BE RETAINED

When you first hear it, you don't know what's hit you. It's like a thousand sirens blasting off together – inside your head. It's the Big Scream, the sound that means Beatlemania from Melbourne to Miami, from Southport to Stockholm.

On Sunday, the experienced walls of the Hippodrome were almost shattered by the Big Scream, when thousands of teenage, and sub-teenage, girls reached the peak of Beatles worship.

Hours before the first of the two Beatles concerts was due to begin, groups of fans began to collect around the Hippodrome.

At first, there were more white-helmeted policemen and magpie-uniformed St. John Ambulance officials than fans. But by the time crush barriers had been erected across Ship Street, near the Hippodrome stage door and Middle Street, the crowd was seven or eight deep.

The fans waited for hours with never a glimpse of their heroes. At times, with apparent reason, there was a frenzy of screaming and cries of 'B.E.A.T.L.E.S. spells Beatles.'

Half a dozen people fainted. One girl got her foot caught under the crush barrier and her screams started another barrage of yelling.

Meanwhile, the four young men concerned had slipped through the main doors in Middle Street from a G.P.O. garage opposite, hardly noticed by the skimpy crowd of ticket-holders and passers-by.

As for the Beatles, the brief, off-stage impression is of nice, friendly boys, casual and a bit scruffy. George Harrison, rather serious and talking about a car accident; Paul, volatile and ready with an instant amusing impression of a Swedish fan; John, hidden behind dark glasses, weary; Ringo – how small he is! – lounging silently against a wall, arms folded, intent and distant at the same time.

Then, in the theatre, the unfortunate artists who came on earlier in the show, contending honourably with shouts of 'We Want the 'Beatles' and some near hysteria that rapidly mounted.

Finally, after an inaudible announcement, the curtain rises on four lonely young men on a vast stage furnished with their complex electronic apparatus.

For the next thirty minutes Bedlam is let loose. The noise is only just endurable. It's like hearing a Beatles record played over a solitary loudspeaker during a football match, acclaimed mostly by women.

The one-note, high-pitched hymn reaches an increasingly frightening volume. A sudden image of the mesmerised crowds at Hitler's rallies flashes through the mind as one watches the eager faces of the worshippers.

Suddenly, it's finished. A girl leaps on the streamer-littered stage and half-embraces Ringo before a quick-footed policeman bundles her away.

Outside, the hopeful crowd is still waiting, this time in Middle Street, but there's only a glimpse of the Beatles through the back of a Black Maria. The extraordinary creations of an idol-hungry generation vanish. And it's all over.

Incidentally, the girl who kissed Ringo was named Beryl Sadler.

While the Beatles were top stars at this time, at the Florida Rooms in Brighton Aquarium, a relatively unknown group calling themselves The High Numbers, appeared intermittently during 1964 and 1965 at Bank Holidays and other times, when not playing clubs in London. Ticket sales were sometimes so poor the Aquarium manager would stand outside giving them away to passers-by in the street! Jimi

Hendrix appeared once too. As The Who, of course, their later name, they would later be forever linked with Brighton, due to the 1979 film *Quadrophenia* being partly filmed in the town and recreating the 1964 Mods and Rockers fighting.

In complete, almost genteel contrast to 'The Beatles Show', the Hippodrome next saw pianist Winifred Atwell, magician David Nixon, singing group The Seekers and vocalist Mark Wynter, playing what would be virtually the theatre's last variety show, although few knew it at the time. Billy J Kramer and the Dakotas appeared soon after, and then another last shot at variety with comedienne Dora Bryan and singer Anne Shelton took place.

The Cliff Richard film, *Wonderful Life* was showing at ABC, the Beatle's film, *A Hard Day's Night* was at the Odeon (and no doubt did tremendous business) and the satirical comedy show, 'Beyond The Fringe' was at the Theatre Royal. Unexpectedly, Old Time Music Hall shows, seen here, started up on the West Pier (in the concert hall, half way down), presented by comedian Alan Gale, who had staged similar shows for nine successive seasons at Margate, Weymouth and Yarmouth. The chairman would be Fred Stone. The cast would include drag artist Gary Williams (of Tisbury Road, Hove), Dale Williams, Patricia Kaye and Pat Howes. This would actually prove to be a

big hit and shows would continue into the 1970s.

The summer of 1964 was when Sussex University's first graduation ceremony took place. Thirty eight undergraduates, who started their courses three years previously, received their degrees in July; eleven men, twenty-seven women.

August 1964 saw the first Brighton Carnival to be held since the war. Organised by the Brighton Lions' Club, it included a procession of decorated floats and a fete in Preston Park, followed by a military tattoo, torchlight processions and an open-air dance on Madeira Drive to the music of eight beat groups. A grand firework display would end what would be 'a memorable day' with the organisers hoping to raise some £5000 for various charities. 'It is expected,' wrote the Brighton and Hove Herald, 'the carnival procession will include 75 decorated floats. Leading it will be the Drum Majorettes and the Carnival Queen, Christine Giddings, who will ride with her attendants in the staff car used by Field Marshall Viscount Montgomery during the later stages of the war. Judging the floats when they line up will be Dame Flora Robson, Dora Bryan and Judy Cornwall'.

The groups at the Madeira Drive dance were all local - The Beat Merchants, Dave Storme and the Tremors, Devlin and the Detours, plus The Headlines. Supporting them were The Debutantes, The Untamed Four, Pete and the Zodiacs and the Ambassadors. One can only wonder what happened to them all and where they are today!

The old Paris Cinema, seen earlier on page 50, was demolished in August 1964. The view here is from Bond Street, looking out from where the stage used to be. A campaign to save the theatre was supported by Sir Laurence Olivier, Sir Ralph Richardson and Charles Laughton, but came to nothing and an office building went up on the site.

Not far away from the old theatre work began in August on the new art college buildings behind Grand parade.

The writing suddenly seemed to be on the wall for live theatre in Brighton during the summer of 1964. Despite the steady and impressive stream of ice-shows, concerts and variety programmes listed so far in this book, not all of them were by any means successful. Rumours about the future of the Hippodrome were rife at this time and when it was announced the repertory company's 1964 season on the Palace Pier would be its last, people began to really sit up. The Theatre Royal of course, continued on its own sweet way, coming up week in, week out with plays, revues, small-scale musicals and the occasional 'show', seemingly oblivious to the upheaval going on all around it.

It was variety shows that were seen as most vulnerable. A sharply written article by Hugo Martin in a September Brighton and Hove

Herald, 'Twilight of the Summer Show', summarised the situation - 'One of the sad things about Brighton in recent years has been the decline of the summer show. The absence of an ice show leaves visitors with the choice of the weekly play at the Theatre Royal, the repertory company at the Palace Pier, 'old time' music hall on the West Pier or the Hippodrome. The Hippodrome show, which stars Dora Bryan, ends tonight. So this week I went along to take a farewell look at what may turn out to be the last summer show ever at this theatre.'

He went on; 'It's a nice, friendly intimate show. But for immediate box office attraction it lacks the big star names featured at nearly all the live shows in Blackpool at the moment and isn't great audience-packing material. No one would be surprised if the Hippodrome made no profit on this summer season. Last year's expensive programme, with lavish and spectacular sets, a large chorus and both Dickie Henderson and Eve Boswell at the top of the bill, was a flop.'

He concluded: 'Holidaymakers in Brighton are not interested in variety. And there are certainly not enough local residents to support top-flight shows on their own. Some of the blame must go to Moss Empires, whose higher officials always seem slightly surprised when you mention the Hippodrome. 'Have we got a theatre in Brighton then?' I was asked by one Moss executive when I telephoned an inquiry to their London-based head office. One can hardly expect the owners to plod on, with little or no return for their capital, trying to find the right formula. Even top draws like the Red Army Choir are so desperately expensive that the theatre shows little profit there.'

'But it is vitally important that the Hippodrome should survive. Brighton hardly deserves the theatres it has, so many care so little for them. One local enthusiast is pressing for a regular Council subsidy for the theatre. This is a matter of priorities, but certainly Brighton makes precious little use of its power to help cultural and entertainment activities in the town.'

But although variety was down, it wasn't quite out and, as we'll see, summer shows would return in a big way - albeit for one last fling - to the Palace Pier in the latter part of the decade - featuring some of the top names in the business.

In August, Gerry and the Pacemakers appeared at the Hippodrome, with the anti-war musical *Oh What A Lovely War* in September (which Richard Attenborough would soon be making a film of in Brighton). September had the Fol-de-Rols company, featuring Jack Tripp. On the Palace Pier the local Brighton and Hove Operatic Society were presenting the Gilbert and Sullivan operetta, 'The Gondoliers'.

In September 1964, a large, detailed model of the proposed Marina was unveiled and the scheme approved by the Corporation, 'in principle.'

In October 1964, designs for a new library, exhibition hall and multi-storey car park, seen on the next page, to be built on the site of Jubilee Street, appeared in the local papers. At a cost of £800,000, the plan was one of the first to acknowledge that conference facilities and exhibition space in the town were limited - basically to just the Dome and Corn Exchange buildings - and that more investment in such amenities was the way forward for the town. The plans were part of a two-year study that recognised the Hotel Metropole's investment in its own conference hall and exhibition space (these were being built at this time) and recommended the Council should have a similar facility at its disposal, catering for some 600 people. One bold aspect of this plan was to block off Church Street to traffic at New Road, creating a continuous line of buildings from North Road, through Church Street, to North Street. Pedestrian access up

Church Street would be under the new library building. Jubilee Street was still lined with houses and shops at this time and the report speculated that £210,000 would be needed to compulsorily purchase those properties not already owned by the Council.

Again, this all became '1960s might-have-been Brighton,' and it wasn't until some forty years later that the recently-opened library took shape on the site.

In October 1964, John, Paul, George and Ringo - the Beatles - played the Hippodrome again. Stalls tickets were again 15/-.

There was no review for the show this time round, but an amusing letter appeared in the Brighton and Hove Herald the following week:

They paid to complain about the Beatles

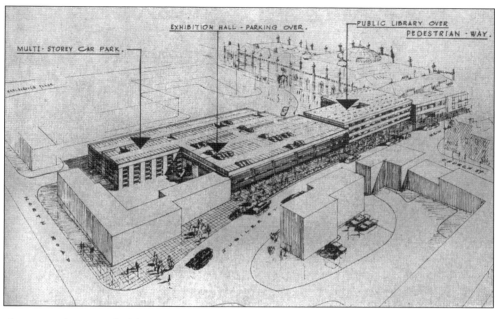

After attending the Beatles' show at the Hippodrome on Sunday and seeing the hundreds of teenage boys and girls waiting outside offering fabulous sums of money for tickets which even then they were unable to obtain, I was quite disgusted by the fact that several of these precious seats had been taken by elderly ladies.

During the entire performance these ladies did nothing but complain about the beat groups, the screaming audience and the inefficiency of the police in charge of the proceedings.

Is it necessary for these people to be so selfish? There was not a single item on the programme which was not along the pop music lines, and the ladies must have known what to expect when they bought their tickets.

Why didn't they leave the tickets for others who were willing to queue all night as we did to see the Beatles and supporting cast?

Do the teenagers go to theatres and operas and shout the performers down with cries of 'Up the Beatles?' No, we leave people who appreciate such forms of entertainment to enjoy it, so why must older people try

BRIGHTON
HIPPODROME

ARTHUR HOWES and
BRIAN EPSTEIN present

The Beatles Show

1st Performance 6-0
SUNDAY
OCTOBER **25**

STALLS
15/-

E**18** CENTRE

TO BE RETAINED

to mar teenage pleasure?

The Beatles' concert turned out to be the very last show of any kind to be staged at the old theatre. The Hippodrome closed immediately after the Beatles' show, with no press announcements as to what the future of the building would be.

In the same letter column was another complaining about students that just has to be included too (from a Robert Tuffnell of Centurion Road):

Students Make Me Mad

It amazes me to see the types studying at the University of Sussex. How on earth did these people win places to a University in the first place?

My fingers itch to cut their hair, give them a good bath (with plenty of disinfectant) and valet their clothes etc.

The majority that I have seen look far from intelligent and I begin to wonder if influence plays a big part in their being at the University?

To continue, I feel sorry for the present generation if the specimens I have seen at the Teacher Training College on the Marine Parade are to be the teachers of these children.

Thank God I am not being educated in 1964!

October was when the political apple cart was well and truly upset in Brighton during the General Election of 1964. This was when Labour's Dennis Hobden won the Kemp Town seat from Conservative David James, by a mere seven votes. And there had to be seven recounts to verify the result. This was the only Sussex seat Labour had ever won and it was held again by Hobden in 1966, but eventually lost in 1970 to Andrew Bowden. Hobden believed his 1964 win had a lot to do with a certain champagne cork he carried around with him. 'After the last election,' he told the press, 'David James asked us to go to a victory party to drink his health and I asked him to give me one of the champagne corks for luck. I have slept with it under my pillow ever since and I shall have it in my pocket when I take my seat in the House. I know it brought me luck.'

In October, the James Bond film Goldfinger opened at the Odeon and everyone would soon be after the Corgi toy model of Bond's Aston Martin DB5 that came out, complete with ejector seat!

In November the Queen returned to Brighton to officially open the new £50,0000 library at Sussex University. It was a wet day and a very amusing incident took place when the Queen paused at a large puddle on a path immediately in front of her. A student stepped forward, whipped off his mackintosh and draped it fully over the water in best Sir Walter Raleigh style. The Queen, smiling, walked over the coat without batting an eyelid, and with a small royal 'thank you', carried on her way!

The Albion Hill Redevelopment Scheme had continued apace all this time and at the end of November 1964 another of the many old pubs in the area closed. This was the 'Live and Let Live' in Richmond Street, run for forty years by Fred Hatton. Previously it had been run by his father and had been in the family since the turn of the century. It's seen on the next page, prior to demolition.

In December 1964, the brewing firm Charringtons announced they would be closing their bottling depot in Kemp Town and moving to Newhaven. These premises were at the corner of St George's Road and Seymour Street (seen here) and were owned by the Kemp Town brewery until 1954, when Charringtons took over. Brewing stopped in 1964. Mr J Shaw, managing director of the firm's south-east operations told the Argus: 'The brewery has been, in local government language, a 'non-conforming user', being in the heart of a residential area and adjacent to the seafront. We are very unwelcome with Brighton Corporation and local residents.' Although the move to Newhaven took place, the old brewery premises, along with a store at the bottom of Sutherland Road weren't demolished until 1970.

Christmas shows and films at the end of the year included a rare pantomime at the Theatre Royal (probably because there was no competition) featuring Dickie Valentine in 'Puss In Boots'. At the Odeon a re-run of the film *The Wizard of Oz* was shown, with Disney's *Snow White and the Seven Dwarfs* at the Regent.

1965

Some Key Events:

January	- Death and state funeral of Sir Winston Churchill.
February	- the millionth Mini comes off the production line - driven by designer Alec Issigonis.
March	- 'Goldie' a golden eagle escapes from London Zoo and is free for thirteen days.
April	- The 'Early Bird' satellite is launched. It begins operating in May.
May	- Edward White performs the first ever 'space walk' during the Gemini IV mission.
July	- Edward Heath becomes leader of the Conservative party.
August	- A ban on TV cigarette advertising in Britain comes into force.
October	- Prime Minister Harold Wilson opens the Post Office Tower in London. Gerry Anderson's Thunderbirds first seen on TV.
November	- Epcot Centre opened in US by Walt Disney (who dies the following month).
December	- Collapse of the 'Sea Gem' oil-rig platform in the North Sea.

No 1 in the music charts at Christmas was 'Day Tripper'/'We Can Work It Out' by The Beatles.

Social snippet - In 1965, there were 37,785 divorces in Britain. Ten years later this number would treble to 120,552.

Film Review: *The Sound of Music* (shown at the Regent)

Schmaltz, like everything else in the entertainment handbook, has its standards. And *The Sound of Music* comes in the superlative bracket of this commodity. It is, therefore, certainly no surprise to learn that the film so softened the hearts of some of Fleet Street's most rock-hard critics that they shame-facedly snivelled their way through most of its press preview, hankies paying soggy testimony to their flow of emotion. It could have been ghastly. All those nuns being angelically secular in their outlook...all those children...and the winsome governess winning the hearts of one and all, including their dictatorial dad. But it isn't. Miraculously, thanks mainly to Julie Andrews determinedly showing Hollywood where to put all its Fair Ladies, it is the perfect family outing for laughter and tears. And of course, there is the music of Rodgers and Hammerstein, masters in high grade schmaltz. This story may not have produced their best works, but who can resist their sweetly pretty 'These Are A Few of My Favourite Things' or their stirring 'Climb Every Mountain'? Not me. Not many.

1965

76

All those who knew Brighton in the 1960s will be expecting chapter and verse in this book on the SS Brighton ice rink in West Street. And so be it...

Opening initially as a swimming pool in 1934, the SS Brighton became an ice rink the following year and served the town as a multi-purpose sports stadium with much of its attraction being its central location. Over the years all manner of events, shows and meetings were held there - tennis, basketball, judo, snooker and wrestling, political and Rotary conferences and any number of spectacular ice shows; it was the Brighton Centre of its day. The ice rink had to be covered for most of these events, of course, and sometimes delegates at meetings complained of chilly feet once the coldness of the ice had worked its way through the boarding and matting laid over the rink!

As already stated, Brighton had its very own ice hockey team, the Brighton Tigers - they started in 1935 - seen here in January 1965, winning the final of the Cobley Cup, against Wembley Lions - a very

hard fought match. 'After a long run of early victories, Tigers really had to put their heads down and hold on', wrote the Brighton and Hove Gazette the following Friday. The score was 9-8 to the Tigers when a penalty clinched the match in their favour. The team photo on the opposite page, dates from the previous season.

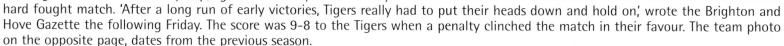

In the cup picture Jackie Dryburgh and Rupe Fresher lead the lap of honour after the match. But, as we've seen, the end of the SS Brighton building was on the cards and the Tigers' glory days were numbered; their last match would be played four months after this picture was taken and the stadium would close later the same year. When the much-awaited new Rank rink finally opened in December 1966, its design proved totally unsuitable for ice hockey, despite the earlier promise of the game being able to continue.

The model here shows what was termed, 'the Metropole's further scheme of redevelopment', unveiled in January 1965; the £5 million plan was passed by Brighton's Planning Committee that month. 'The southeast corner and the Cannon Place frontage', reported the Brighton and Hove Herald, 'including the old post office, will be replaced by luxury flats and new kitchens for the

hotel. At street level there will be a grill room, coffee lounge and patisserie designed to attract not only summer visitors but winter ones as well. In the patisserie, where the bread for the whole development, including the exhibition halls, is baked, it is hoped that the smell of freshly baked bread and French pastries served with hot chocolate will tempt people in even the coldest weather. A bank and a florist's shop which can be reached from the hotel will also be incorporated as a service for conference delegates.'

Councillor I Dudeney, chairman of the Planning Committee, said: ' We are very pleased. From our point of view a very unsightly corner will disappear. The plans will round off the Metropole development and they are in keeping with the five star hotel class that the Metropole is aiming to obtain.' However, this corner project was where AVP's money must have run out, as the plan never came to fruition.

In February 1965, a new £380,000 grandstand at Brighton Race Course was being built, seen opposite, scheduled to be ready for the first race meeting of May.

'Plans for ending traffic congestion at Preston Circus are being considered by the town council's Planning Committee,' reported the Argus in March. 'A number of schemes including a flyover to take east-west traffic across the main London-Brighton road have been discussed.' A flyover would have solved the problem of tailbacks to St Peter's Church at a stroke, but was another scheme that came to nothing (no designs of what it might have looked like were produced). It was, though, the start of plans that would see a complete re-routeing of traffic in the area. 'It seems likely,' the report said, 'that measures would include one-way traffic in such roads as Viaduct Road and Upper Lewes Road. In these circumstances, the corner of site of Ditchling Road, with the associated routes Viaduct Road, Rosehill Terrace and Union Road, might well become a critical point in the traffic pattern of the town.'

Also in March 1965, the Corporation announced it would be closing Cobden Road slipper baths. These were basically public baths that could be used by anyone who didn't have a bath in their house, something that was becoming increasingly a thing of the past in the town. They were called slipper baths because of their shape. 'Because North Road Baths should have the capacity to provide the total slipper bath requirements now existing in the borough and which is still dwindling,' reported the Brighton and Hove Herald, 'although at a much lower rate than during the past 15 years, Brighton Council is being recommended by the Entertainments and Publicity Committee to close the Cobden Road slipper baths from March 31 next year. At that time, too, it is suggested the future of the slipper baths at North Road and Park Street should be again considered.' All three bath buildings wouldn't actually close until the 1970s. The Cobden Road premises still stand as flats.

In the spring of 1965, the longest continuous run of any film in Brighton began. This was *The Sound of Music,* which started at the Regent on 15th April and ran there for just over a year until 25th May 1966. What film lasts so long today?

In May, Brighton General Hospital was 100 years old. Some 300 members of staff celebrated its centenary with a dance and cabaret evening at the Royal Pavilion, which ran well into the early hours of the following morning. Every baby born at the hospital within the centenary week received a silver spoon embossed with the hospital's coat of arms.

Woolworth's store in London Road - seen here with Cheapside to its left - was bought by the firm of Sainsbury in May 1965, for £190000. Sainsbury's had a small shop next door (it had been there for sixty years), which would be rebuilt and extended over the Woolworth's site, opening in 1969. Woolworth's would move to bigger premises, further along London Road.

Another plan for a new Town Hall, this time standing on King's Road, was suddenly on the drawing board in mid-1965. The site chosen, seen below, was between Black Lion Street (left) and Little East Street (right) and would involve demolishing the old 1830-31 Town Hall. The aerial view, probably taken the year before, shows the site the new buildings would occupy.

Seafront offices and a 1901 market building, which stood mostly demolished at this time and in use as a car park, would also be removed under the scheme. Nothing came of this plan, but the site would be redeveloped in the 1980s, with the building of the Ramada Hotel and new civic centre at the rear, the old Town Hall being retained though.

Clearing the site for the Churchill Square shopping centre - a view taken in the summer of 1965; eighteen streets and courtyards in all were demolished for the project - over a long period of time - and the original topography of the area was obliterated.

Although being, in most peoples' minds, the iconic 1960s building project, ideas for redeveloping the area between West Street and the seafront had begun as long ago as 1929, when the Corporation bought a large redundant brewery near the seafront end. This site was cleared in 1932, followed by a number of houses demolished as slum clearance, just before World War II. Other old shops, houses and workshops also came down as opportunities arose, but the war put a stop to any large-scale clearance and redevelopment. In the 1950s, the patchy remains of the area had become very run down, some parts derelict, finally leading to the 1959 plans and eventual redevelopment of the whole site between Western Road and the

seafront during the 1960s.

The photograph shows only half of Grenville Place left standing (behind the long hoarding) and beyond, left, the shops of Western Road can be made out. Upper Russell Street ran from the line of buildings at the bottom of the picture, in the centre, diagonally across to the right, and then swung northwards past the lines of cars, up towards Western Road.

The other view looking down from the Grand Hotel, taken at exactly the same time, is further south. The main building under construction, in the foreground, is what was then referred to as the Cannon Street car park, as it covered the site of Cannon Street, lost in the 1950s. The car park would be rushed through, so it would be ready to use for those attending the Brighton Toy Fair of early 1966. In the middle distance, on the right, is the Cannon Street brewery, which would be demolished in 1969. The origins of this brewery went back to the 1820s. Between the brewery and St. Paul's Church,

is St. Paul's School, the entrance to which was in Little Russell Street, demolished as part of the same site, the children transferring to their new building in Centurion Road. In between buildings left of centre, the cream frontage of the Academy Cinema can just be seen. This operated from 1911 to 1973. To the right, cars are on the site seen in the previous picture.

Right at the other end of the shopping scale, the demise of the small corner shop throughout the post-war period is epitomised by this view, left, of the early 1960s (exact date unknown). This old grocers stood at the corner of Carlton Hill (left) and William Street (foreground), being typical of the scores of small shops that were once common in the area. It was obviously soon to close and would be demolished as part of the new John Street Police HQ site. As in most small shops like it, a 'slate' system operated for regulars, where purchases weren't initially paid for, but were listed over a weekly period (put 'on the slate'), then all paid for when the week was up. This was the kind of shop, where, in its heyday, you took your own bottle in to buy something like vinegar and a jam jar for jam. Everything was loose and had to be weighed and put into paper bags. Sugar, rice, washing soda and dried fruit came in sacks and had to be scooped out. Soap was in a long bar and what you wanted was cut off.

The other small shop seen here, standing in Sydney Street, has 'self service' as the shape of things to come. 'Green Shield Stamps' were being given away with purchases at this time (the more you spent, the more stamps you were given), enabling shoppers to choose gifts from a catalogue in exchange for books of stamps. Tesco, of course, would eventually build into one of the largest supermarket chains in the country, opening huge 'megastores' (like the recent one in Church Road, Hove), changing the whole nature of shopping. In the autumn of 2004 (while this section of the book was being compiled) it was established that for every £8 spent in High Street shopping, £1 went to Tesco - that's some progression over the forty years since this tiny fledgling shop operated.

July also saw another Brighton Lion's Carnival take place (following the huge success of the one the previous year). Eighty floats were in the parade with 150 sideshows in Preston Park. One new attraction in the arena at the park was an unusual dance display. 'THE thing in America and Australia is Go-Go dancing', said the organisers, 'and it is beginning to catch on in England. See how it's done with a demonstration by the Carnaby Go-Go School.' There also was a 'rave' on Madeira Drive in the evening, to round the carnival off, plus a firework display.

Back to large stores again, in August 1966, Selfridges, the well-known London retailer, announced they had reserved premises in the Churchill Square complex to open their first out of London store. This was revoked a year later, when the site was said to be 'unsuitable'.

In August legendary screen diva Marlene Dietrich appeared at the Theatre Royal. She had the audience at her feet on opening night, according to the local press. They cheered her 'jerky, outrageous 'Backroom Boys', laughed delightedly at the sing-song 'Lola' from 'The Blue Angel', chuckled at the enormous wink that went with 'The Laziest Girl In Town' and shouted for more after 'Falling In Love Again.'' She would make a return visit in November 1966, when, it has to be said, the review wasn't quite so glowing!

Summer entertainment in Brighton 1965 also saw 'Take A Trip' on the Palace Pier, a variety show starring Jack Tripp and Kathleen West, presented by Miles Byrne.

In September 1965, the Home Secretary, Sir Frank Soskice, officially opened the new police station in John Street. The view below, left, shows it nearing completion a few months earlier.

The last event held at the SS Brighton was the Conservative Party Conference of 1965, which ran from 13th-16th October. The picture here dates from the 17th October, when the TV crew covering the event were moving their equipment out - and the demolition gang were about to move in. On the left, at the seafront corner of West Street, the Top Rank complex is under construction.

The model showing the original extent of Rank's entertainment centre (seen at top of the next page) shows how it was to cover the site of the SS Brighton (the section of model on the right), housing shops and a restaurant. Although the SS Brighton was demolished, nothing was built on the site and the area remained

undeveloped as a 'temporary' car park for virtually twenty-five years, until the building of the Oak hotel (now the Quality), in the early 1990s.

In early October 1965, the Mayor, Alderman Dudley Baker, laid the foundation stone for a new Waterworks Department building at Falmer. This new complex, ready in the summer of 1967, at a cost £340,000, would centralise the programming system for Brighton's eleven pumping stations, including the three automated ones at Patcham, Mile Oak and Sompting.

More watery matters! The 1960s were the decade when plans for the marina at Black Rock finally came to fruition. As an idea there was actually nothing new in this proposal. For the best part of 200 years there had been schemes for some kind of harbour at Brighton, but the basic problem of siting and engineering a huge structure that would, in actual fact, have to stand in the open sea, had proved too daunting or too costly. Remember how quickly the 1961 plan had been dropped - the one utilizing the Banjo Groyne.

But from 1963, following the initial proposals by Henry Cohen, a Brighton petrol station proprietor, some twelve years of enquiries, site changes, town polls, Parliamentary Bills and ever escalating costs took place before the Brighton Marina at Black Rock started taking shape.

The picture here shows a 1965 model of the Marina, with Henry Cohen standing centre. It's not the same as the model mentioned earlier. At a cost of some £9 million, as well as berths for 3,000 boats, it was to have some forty attractions and features including a theatre, cinema, an oceanarium, sports centre, ice rink (to replace the SS Brighton), tennis courts, a new market for local fishermen, plus a large amount of residential accommodation, in order that the Marina would, 'live twelve months of the year and not become dormant in the off-season'.

It was obviously extremely audacious, attractive and controversial. 'The greatest and most exciting scheme that had ever come before the Council,' said the Chairman of the Planning Committee, Ivan Dudeney. Yet a curt letter in the Daily Telegraph of September 1964 had said it would just end up 'a conglomeration of hotels and a shantytown. There will be petrol stations, fumes,

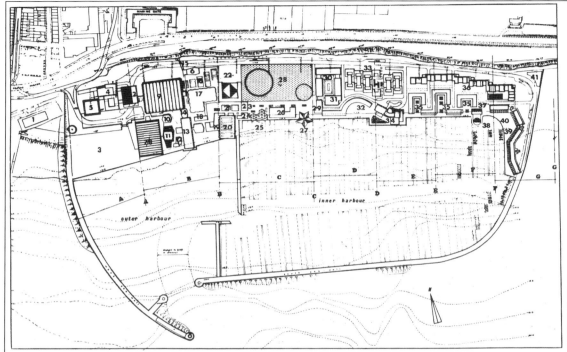

tar and litter. You have the sea today. You will not have it afterwards.' The plan here shows all the attractions the new marina was to offer.

Details of the Top Rank entertainment centre appeared in October 1965. It was announced that 'squares', 'with-its' and ballroom enthusiasts would be drawn from all over the south coast by its state-of-the-art attractions. The main feature was the balconied octagonal ballroom, which could be put to a variety of uses 'at the touch of a button' (seen opposite, above nearing completion). The chequer-board glass ceiling, with its changing rainbow lighting patterns, could be lowered 'in seconds' from its normal position to within 12ft 6ins of the dance floor, to give a more intimate atmosphere suitable for small functions. The band stage was revolving and could be moved to the centre of the dance floor so dancers could surround it. The black and orange

KEY
1. Existing Black Rock Swimming Pool. 2. Petrol Filling station, offices over. 3. Power Boat centre, showrooms, maintenance and offices. 4. Kiosks. 5. Marina Administration offices. 6. News Theatre. 7. & 8. Bowling, Rollcurling rink, Dancing and restaurant. 9. Ice rink. 10. Public house. 11. Dinghy park or open air ice rink (winter). 12. Children's play area. 13. Hotel/Motel. 14. Private arts club theatre. 15. Footbridge from upper Cliff Walk. 16. Youth Centre and children's recreational area. 17. Main theatre and cinema. 18. Shops – general. 19. Marina shops. 20. Boatyard and slips. 21. Sports shop. 22. Sports centre with open-air tennis courts. 23. Public house. 24. Fishmarket, angling club, and fishermen's jetty. 25. Yacht club. 26. Speciality restaurant. 27. Casino/night club. 28. Oceanarium or luxury swimming pool and oceanarium. 29. Public house. 30. Shops and offices. 31. Supermarket. 32. High-class residential accommodation with marina facilities. 33. Two storey residential accommodation. 34. Luxury Hotel (50 bedrooms). 35. Two storey residential units. 36. Ziggurat flats. 37. Public house. 38. Luxury Restaurant. 39. Boatel. 40. Boatel restaurant. 41. Cafe.

ballroom furniture was chosen from an exhibition at the Design Centre in London and a panel of 'women experts' had been asked to help design the powder rooms, which had soft flattering pink lights behind white silk walls. 'The sound amplification is the most modern in the country,' it was stated. 'It can mix up to ten microphones simultaneously, serving the orchestra, solo instrumentalists, vocalists or the announcer. Pleasant background music would be piped to the buffet areas and powder rooms.' All the food served in the suite would be cooked on the premises under the supervision of chief chef Monsieur Francois, who had spent fourteen years at the Metropole Hotel, three years at English's and four at the Sackville Hotel in Hove.

In November 1965, at Curry's, the electrical store in York Place, 'Britain's lowest-priced TV' was on sale for 59 guineas (so just over £60). The screen size was 23 inches.

In November it was announced that two experimental houses, seen above, built in 1922-23 entirely of metal, would be demolished. These stood in Queen's Park Road, near the Elm Grove junction, and were commercially known as Weir steel houses. They were the only ones built in the town, as a trial during the slump following World War I, when there was a shortage of traditional building materials. They didn't actually come down until the very end of the decade.

The Top Rank building finally opened in November 1965; the picture here shows the exterior facing the seafront nearing completion. The design of the Top Rank complex provoked wild hostility because it was basically just a concrete box and architecturally at odds with all the other buildings on the

seafront, particularly the nearby Grand Hotel. The lack of any detailing, to relieve the plain façade, was particularly criticised, leading later to one small window being installed on the seafront side. The buildings previously on the site of the Top Rank building are seen on the opposite page.

Initially, it was just a large dance hall - the Top Rank Suite - with bar areas, but just over a year later, the promised ice rink and bowling alley opened. The ice rink (seen here) was welcomed as a replacement for the SS Brighton but, as already said, was unsuitable for ice hockey matches, to the complete dismay of Brighton Tiger fans; it eventually proved to be financially unsuccessful. It could, however, double as a conference centre, holding some 6,000 delegates as planned.

Those who remember the opening of the Top Rank Brighton Suite, as it was now officially called, might like to be reminded of the full itinerary for the week it came into operation. On 8th November an 'Open House' was held, where the management invited the public to 'view the Suite free' between 7.30 and 10.30 pm. An Opening Charity Ball, in conjunction with the Sussex Association of Boys' Clubs would be held two days later, between 8pm and 2am. Tickets for this were £2/2/-. A free under-16's session was offered between 9.30 am and 12 noon on Saturday 13th, followed by another 'Open House' until 4.00 pm. In the evening came the first 'Night Out' dancing session, from 7.30 until midnight. The cost of this was 7/6. The weekly programme then would be up and running, with 'Sunday Date' at 4/6 (7.00-11.00pm), Mondays, Wednesdays, Fridays and Saturday afternoons were reserved for private functions or special events, Tuesdays would be 'Disc Date' at 3/- (7.00-11.00pm), Thursday was 'Party Night' from 7.30pm-12.00 midnight and Saturday had an under sixteen session from 9.30am until 12 noon for 1/6, then in the evening, 7.30 until midnight was 'Night Out'. Dancing was to Syd Dean and his Music. Fully licensed bars would be operating.

In November 1965, the film *The Guns Of Navarone* was showing at the Odeon, *My Fair Lady* was at the Astoria, with *The Sound of Music* continuing at the Regent.

November also saw a row over whether fluoride should be put into Brighton's water supply come to an important vote. This was a major issue virtually everywhere at this time. A key meeting to decide the matter saw much heckling from the public gallery at the town hall; 'Who are we to force people to take a drug?' was one shouted comment. The eventual vote was thirteen in favour, fifty-two against.

Brighton and Hove Albion played two extraordinary matches in November 1965, which have now entered the record books as the highest scoring home games in the club's entire history. First they beat Wisbech 10-1, then, later the same month, beat Southend 9-1! Was it something in the water?!

Despite these overwhelming victories, the 1960s were pretty dismal years for the Albion, where they crashed down to Division 2, then 3, finally 4, only reviving slightly at the end of the decade and getting back into Division 3 again. But glory days were ahead of course. Their first match in Division 1 would come in August 1979 and their legendary game in the FA Cup Final, at Wembley, in May 1983, holding titans Manchester United to a 1-1 draw was the stuff of dreams. Sadly, they lost the replay.

'Work on the complex details of the multi-million pound, 14-acre Churchill Square site, stretching from Western Road to the Sea Front is going smoothly and to schedule,' reported the Brighton and Hove Herald in late November 1965. 'Brighton's Borough Engineer and Surveyor, Mr Dennis Howe, said yesterday that he was very happy with the progress made and the dream Brighton has cherished for so long, of an elegant, yet practical, town's centre - a model of town planning in the contemporary idiom - is steadily becoming a reality.'

Advertisements for the Ritz in West Street at this time showed an increase in the amusements on offer. There were now 'bingo, bowls, shooting, tattoo, palmist, a café and all the latest automatic machines.'

Not surprisingly, the closure of both the SS Brighton and the Hippodrome left a big hole in seasonal shows in Brighton over the 1965 Christmas period. The Brighton and Hove Operatic Society was staging the only pantomime to be seen, 'Aladdin', at the Dome. Cinemas responded though by screening a succession of family films, including several Disney reruns such as *Peter Pan, Snow White* and *Mary Poppins*; *The Wizard of Oz* was also being shown. The only new film for the season was *The Great Race* at the Astoria.

A new bike for a youngster at Christmas 1965? A 'Sunbeam Jolly Jester' tricycle would be £4/19/6 and a 'Raleigh Rebel' (now why did they chose that name?) would cost £18/5/-. An RSW 16 (whatever that meant) could be had for 29 guineas. This last bike was 'for all sorts of people, from trend-setting paper boys to joyful tycoons.'

1966

Some Key Events:

February	- US troops in Vietnam now numbered 190,000.
March	- John Lennon of the Beatles makes his infamous remark in an Evening Standard interview: 'We're more popular than Jesus'.
April	- Labour win the General Election. Harold Wilson continues as Prime Minister.
May	- Life imprisonment for 'Moor's Murderers' Myra Hindley and Ian Brady.
June	- Over a quarter of a million troops now in Vietnam.
July	- England win the World Cup, beating Germany 4-2 at Wembley.
September	- First arrest for Great Train Robbery - Ronald Edwards.
October	- The Aberfan disaster in South Wales, when a massive pile of pit slurry swamps a school. 116 children and 28 adults are killed.
December	- Government begin negotiations to allow Rhodesia to become independent.

No 1 in the music charts at Christmas was 'The Green, Green Grass Of Home' by Tom Jones.

Social Snippet - Remember these hit singles in the UK charts for 1966? These Boots Are Made For Walking (Nancy Sinatra), Nineteenth Nervous Breakdown (The Rolling Stones), Dedicated Follower of Fashion and Sunny Afternoon (The Kinks), God Only Knows and Sloop John B (The Beach Boys) and Uptight (Stevie Wonder). Top Albums included Rubber Soul and Revolver (The Beatles), Best Of The Beach Boys, Aftermath (The Rolling Stones) and the soundtracks for the movies Dr Zhivago and The Sound of Music.

Local Film Review: *Doctor Zhivago* (shown at the Astoria) -
When a celebrated book is made into a film comparisons are usually odious - but *Doctor Zhivago* has two wide advantages. First, although the book has been widely acclaimed few people have read right the way through it; and secondly, director David Lean has supplemented Pasternak's masterpiece with scenes of pure cinematic splendour. Carlo Ponti, the producer, took a huge gamble by bringing this story to the screen with the aid of such youthful stars as Tom Courtenay, Julie Christie and Geraldine Chaplin. That this film is a masterpiece in its own right is more than due to the efforts of these three, who celebrate their arrival at screen maturity.

In January 1966 the cost of the Marina was put at £10 million. Several backers for the project had emerged by now, including Sir Robert McAlpine's construction company and the Allied Land and Investment Company. Shell Mex and BP Ltd 'had already advanced a considerable sum of money' for the project. Henry Cohen would be chairman of the Marina Company.

The annual Toy Fair was held at various venues in January 1966, again showing the need for one large exhibition space in Brighton.

In February, The Princes News Theatre, in North Street, changed from showing continuous programmes of shorts and cartoons, to presenting 'continental' art films.

February 1966 - the photographs opposite show the SS Brighton ice rink being demolished. The interior view shows the floor taken up revealing the shallow end of the old swimming pool of 1934. Part of the Grand Hotel can be seen top left and the chimney of an old brewery building in Russell Street is on the right. As detailed earlier, the site wasn't developed as intended and the empty site became a car park, staying that way for nearly a quarter of a century. While the SS Brighton was coming down, the Metropole's exhibition halls were going up; work was well under way with them at this time.

In February, the popular 'Tuesday at the Dome' variety show, organised by Douglas Reeve (seen below), celebrated its 1000th performance; the first had been in July 1946.

In February, the Borough Engineer, Dennis Howe, faced ten hours of hostile questioning at a ministerial enquiry for a

proposed road scheme at Black Rock, which would widen several roads and create an underpass to the Marina. The cost would be £830,000 and it would be carried out even if the Marina wasn't built, 'to meet the seafront traffic problems of that area.' It was stated that the widening of Riflebutt Road was part of an old 1930 plan and it was 'inevitable' that Arundel Road should get similar treatment. Mr Howe stated that 'the advent of the Marina had only brought the plan forward.' One interesting aspect of the proceedings was when Michael Mann, representing Brighton Corporation, answered questions on Brighton's title to the foreshore. He said the town had bought the land between high and low water marks, from the Crown, in July 1936 for £806, with no 'restrictive covenants'. However, no buildings could be erected on the site without permission from the Board of Trade.

In February, the new James Bond film *Thunderball* was showing to packed houses at the Odeon.

A fire broke out in a large five-storey furniture warehouse in Queen's Road during February, 1966, seen opposite. Ninety firemen from four brigades fought the blaze and thousands of pounds worth of stock was destroyed. The following month, Waitrose, in Western Road, opened, advertised as 'Brighton's Biggest Food Store.' There was also a freak blizzard in April, the first since 1958.

By March 1966, Brighton Square, in the Lanes, was virtually complete. 'Steadily increasing in popularity as the new shopping centre of the town is Brighton Square,' announced an advertising feature in the Brighton and Hove Herald. 'Situated right in the heart of the famous Lanes but easily accessible from North Street and East Street and all areas adjacent to the Town Hall. Only a short time ago the one and a half acre site was a waste of dilapidated buildings hidden at points by unsightly hoardings. Demolition commenced and soon there emerged a scheme of reconstruction, gay, imaginative and harmonising delightfully with its surroundings. The shops provide a wide cross-section and include ladies' fashions, gifts, children's wear, a drug store, shoes, optician, furnishings and baby wear. An outstanding feature is the proposed restaurant with its terrace roof where patrons can sit in the summer sunshine.'

At Easter, disturbances by Mods and Rockers hit the headlines again - 'Gangs of youths beating up a man near the Clock Tower...slapping a honeymooner who protected his wife...cafes forced to close...snarling police dogs on the Sea Front.' Alderman Gerald Fitzgerald, at a subsequent Council debate, stated, 'the cure for these thugs is discipline.

Give these youths a short period of discipline, a short back-and-sides, good uniforms and you will turn them into good citizens.' An incident on the Easter Sunday was when a Rocker and his pillion passenger, riding a bike on Madeira Drive, were surrounded by twenty or so 'umbrella-waving Mods' who chanted 'kill these Rockers' and one struck the passenger. Two were arrested and a £10 fine imposed on both. A sixteen-year-old grammar school boy from Bristol was fined £10 for carrying a knuckle-duster and a further £20 for possessing drugs. Two other sixteen-year-olds, caught in possession of 'French Blues', were also fined £20 each. Further fines imposed on others included £10 for insulting language, £5 for obstruction and £5 for threatening behaviour. The Council debate ended with a motion drawn up urging the government to provide legislation so the Bank Holiday troublemakers could be sentenced to periods of enforced work for the public good.

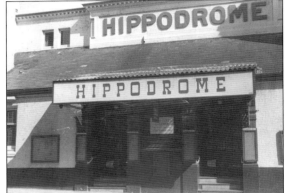

The Hippodrome in nearby Middle Street stood empty at this time, following closure after the second Beatles' concert. A deal with Charles Forte, to turn it into a £250,000 'Talk Of The Town' nightspot fell through but the theatre was adapted into a TV studio early in 1966 (seen below). This followed the TV company ATV taking over Moss Empires interests, owners of the Hippodrome. The venture was short-lived, but several 1960s icons were recorded performing there (in May) including Freddie and the Dreamers, Dusty Springfield and rising star Liza Minnelli, daughter of Judy Garland (all seen below).

In June 1966, the Bishop of Lewes, the Rt. Rev. J H L Morrell, laid the foundation stone for a new St Paul's School, in Centurion Road, replacing the old St Paul's school building off West Street (seen on the next page), which would be demolished as part of the West Street Redevelopment Scheme. The cost was more than £128,000, making it one of the most expensive church schools ever built by the Chichester diocese.

June also saw the promise of 608 more parking meters being introduced to the town.

In July 1966, the Argus ran an article on Brighton's Cold Store and Meat Market, that had recently closed in Russell Street; the site, when cleared, would become part of the Churchill Square car park area. The interest here was the building the store and market occupied. It was originally an underground church, reportedly the only one of its kind in the country. This was the 1878 Church of the Resurrection, funded by the formidable Arthur Douglas Wagner, who with his father built eleven churches in the town. It was to be a chapel of ease for the overcrowded St Paul's in West Street, but when told of an injunction, served by a neighbouring brewery, that he could not built above a certain height due to an old bye-law of 'ancient lights' (basically not blocking out other people's windows) it was a case of not building up, but building down, with huge excavations being made to accommodate the bulk of the building.

Wagner died in 1902 and the church was sold off eight years later. In 1912, because of its unique underground location, it became the town's main cold meat store, capable of storing 350 tons of meat. This moved to new, modern premises at Hollingdean in June 1966 and the old church became a temporary bottle store for the adjoining brewery. The building finally came down in 1969.

Summer shows and films in 1966 included 'Summer Cocktails' on the Palace Pier with Alec Pleon and his London Company (seen here), while the Theatre Royal continued largely with plays, including Agatha Christie's 'The Hollow'. *Doctor Zhivago* was the big film at the Astoria, *The Sound of Music* was now at the Academy, the Regent had *Those Magnificent Men In Their Flying Machines* showing and Odeon had *Duel at Diablo*. The Curzon was showing *Room At The Top*, while the Continental had *Nude Camera* and *Rendezvous at Midnight*. Dr Zhivago was another film scheduled for an amazingly long run in Brighton - some forty weeks. Staring in June, it ran continuously until May the following year, then returned for a rerun, running from August to October.

In July came the news that Brighton Corporation was planning to compulsorily purchase the entire ten-acre Kemp Town Railway site, seen here, from British

Rail - and turn the station and yard area between Freshfield and Sutherland Roads into a housing estate. Ideas to make the actual line into a roadway (spectacularly passing through a tunnel which was three-quarters of a mile long and then over Lewes Road on a massive viaduct - now gone) were dismissed as the minimum legal road width of twenty-eight feet would not be met (the trackway was an average sixteen feet wide). Also, the tunnel had no suitable ventilation. It would be several more years before there was any real movement on this plan and nothing was built on the site until the early 1970s, when the first part of the Freshfield Industrial Estate was laid out.

In August 1966, a film studio in St Nicholas Road closed after operating for eighteen years. This was originally known as Film Studios (Brighton) Ltd, and could be hired by any company needing recording facilities in Brighton. In the 1960s, it mainly produced adverts for TV. With the area around scheduled for residential development, the owners - Wynne Film Productions Ltd - sold up, intending to move to London.

Also in August came the news that one of Brighton's most centrally located churches was about to close and be demolished. This was the really ancient and historic Countess of Huntingdon's Church in North Street, which was rebuilt several times during its 200 years of life. 'The lovely white church,' ran an article in the Brighton Herald, 'was built to hold 1500 people. But congregations have steadily dwindled and today average about sixteen people. The main reason for the closure, though, is damage to the church fabric, with a crack in the spire, which would be very costly to repair.'

The cracked tower began to tilt and was taken down in 1969 (seen here); North Street had to be closed to traffic for this to happen. The main body of the church would remain until 1972 and a plaque inside the doorway of the modern building occupying the site is all that's left to mark what was one of Brighton's most unique churches.

'The world's first double deck bus with a one-man crew comes into operation in Brighton...' reported the Argus in early September 1966. This bore 'Pay As You Enter' signs and had an 'electronic eye' to check the number of people boarding. 'The driver conductor operates an electric ticket and change machine,' the Argus continued, 'and he has a microphone and special mirrors to keep in touch with passengers. The driver-conductors will receive 16% extra pay, which puts them in the £1000-a-year class.' In the picture, typist Linda Powell tries out the system, the bus driver being a Mr H Smith.

September 1966; the area between Edward Street and Albion Hill is now dominated by six high-rise blocks (later described as 'infinitely uncivilised,' by the Brighton historian, Antony Dale), seen under construction on previous pages. As with the Churchill Square project, a large number of streets and courtyards had now gone forever and the area today bears no topographical relation to how it used to be. Four-storey housing has gone up in the Albion Street area and the triangle of land in the distance, to the left, is all that remains of a small dairy farm, which operated from 1858 until 1934. The houses of the Tarner estate can also be seen - built

just before World War II - and in the foreground it's obviously playtime at the Margaret Hardy School for girls, part of what used to be the York Place Elementary Schools, off York Place. The Fawcett School for boys was also housed in this building at this time, but both would soon move to sites well out of central Brighton.

Lord Cohen of Brighton died in September 1966. He became mayor of Brighton in the mid-1950s and could claim many achievements; he's best remembered for founding what would become the Alliance Building Society from a small office near the Clock Tower back in the 1920s. Like Herbert Carden in the 1930s, he had a 'grand plan' for Brighton, which included - back in 1951 - ideas for new conference facilities and shopping arcade between West Street and Russell Square. One attractive idea of his was to extend the chain of gardens running through the centre of Brighton, so that 'from Knoyle Road to the sea, a chain of gardens would run right through the valley of the town.'

September 1966 saw the first full-page advertisement appear for Sussex Heights, with the heading – 'All the luxuries of modern living.' Ninety-one two-bedroom flats were now available, twenty-four one-bedroom. 'Substantially constructed of reinforced concrete,' the advert continued, 'and combining every modern design feature, Sussex Heights is beautifully finished with attractive Italian Mosaic facing, and is built to the very highest standards. Approached through an elegantly appointed, close-carpeted entrance hall with marble-cased columns, it is served by two fast, fully automatic passenger lifts of the latest design.' This first advert didn't give prices, but others, of January the following year, did: a one-bedroomed flat was £5,450, a two-bedroomed flat £5,950. Features pointed up included 'large elegant living rooms; magnificent views from every room; superbly equipped, ultra-modern kitchens; spacious sun balconies; fitted wardrobes in all bedrooms; 125 year leases; garage facilities.' The picture here shows Sussex Heights nearing completion earlier in the year. The Metropole's exhibition halls are also being finished, seen opposite the lorry.

In October 1966 a large group of Young Socialists from Sussex University marched along King's Road (seen on the next page) to protest at the way the Labour Party, holding their 64th conference at the Top Rank building that month, were handling several key issues at this time. These included unemployment, particularly in the car industry and a wage and price freeze the Wilson government were about to impose. Many were condemning the Vietnam War too, where some 350 US personnel were being killed per week. Students at the University were becoming more militant now and protesters seemed to be everywhere that week, with heckling and abuse thrown at any opportunity; Prime Minister Harold Wilson and foreign secretary George Brown were even shouted down while reading the lessons at Dorset Gardens

Methodist Church, and the Brighton and Hove Herald reported: 'This week we have had the sorry sight of the Prime Minister and, to a lesser degree, Mr. George Brown, flanked by a heavy bodyguard of both uniformed and plain-clothes detectives.'

October 1966 marked the centenary of the West Pier. Big celebrations? Not a bit of it - and further proof that Brighton has never really known how to celebrate its extraordinary past. 'Complete modernisation is planned by AVP Industries Ltd', announced the local press, 'who bought ninety percent of the company's shares last year. There will be an improved entrance, a different façade, a covered walk on top of the central walk to give panoramic views of Brighton, a small playhouse for summer shows plus a theatre and a clubhouse with sunbathing facilities to replace the Ocean Restaurant.' All this was pie in the sky and the director of AVP, Harold Poster, would later go on record as saying he wasn't prepared to spend his shareholder's money on upgrading the pier.

Also in October 1966, it was announced that the South Eastern Gas Board were moving out of their premises in West Street, to offices in Grand Parade. The interest here was the old building they occupied, one of only two early nineteenth-century houses that survived in the whole of West Street (today, in 2005, it's the only one left). These premises were connected with the gas industry in Brighton since the 1880s and before nationalisation were the HQ for the old Brighton, Hove and Worthing Gas Company. Many will remember going there to pay their bills!

In November, the 'topping out' ceremony was undertaken on Cavendish House, a fifteen-storey block of flats on King's Road, west of Regency Square, with 1966 coins pressed into the cement by the director of the developers. The block contained forty-one flats, selling in the region of £10,000 each, with £25,000 expected for the top penthouse suite. Later publicity for the block - when the flats were ready for occupancy - would describe it as 'a residential development of charm and distinction.'

November 1966 also brought news of the Council's newest housing

1966

development. This was the £1 million scheme at Whitehawk, where five tower blocks containing 258 flats were nearing completion. Two blocks were already occupied, two other blocks were complete and the fifth would be ready by mid-December. Work had started in January 1964, the builders averaging eight flats per week. Part of the design brief was that the completed blocks should not extend above the horizon, not for aesthetic reasons, but because if built higher, they would obstruct the view of the racecourse from the nearby grandstand.

December 1966 was when Top Rank's new ice rink and sixteen-lane bowling centre (seen below) opened to the public, extending the attractions of their new seafront entertainment centre. 1,500 pairs of skates (red for men, white for women) were stocked for hire, with, initially, seven instructors, led by former figure-skating champion Valda Osborn. She'd been British figure-skating champion in 1952 and 1953, also European champion in 1953.

Christmas shows and films for 1966 included 'The Fols Christmas Show' at the Theatre Royal, with Freddie Sales, Joan Mann, and featuring 'Jimmie Currie's Waterfalls of Scotland' - where a cascading mountain waterfall scene appeared in seconds on stage. Films included *Thunderbirds Are Go* at the Odeon, *Khartoum* at the Regent, with *Doctor Zhivago* continuing at the Astoria.

1967

Some Key Events:

January	- Donald Campbell killed on Lake Coniston attempting new water speed record.
March	- First North Sea gas comes ashore at Easingham, County Durham.
April	- Boxer Muhammad Ali refuses military service.
May	- Stunt rider Evel Knievel jumps over sixteen cars on his motorbike at the Ascot Speedway in Gardena, California.
June	- The Beatle's album, 'Sgt. Pepper's Lonely Heart's Club Band' is released.
July	- Decriminalisation of homosexuality in Britain.
August	- The Government bans pirate radio stations.
September	- Radio 1 is launched.
October	- A Bill legalising abortion is passed in Parliament.
December	- Unveiling of Concorde in Toulouse, France.

No 1 in the music charts at Christmas was 'Hello Goodbye' by the Beatles.

Social Snippet - A 'consumer research' report showed that in 1967 Britain, the fridge was thought to be the most useful kitchen gadget, with a dishwasher considered least useful.

Local Film Review; *Carry On Don't Lose Your Head.* (shown at the Odeon)

What a relief, after sitting through some pretentiously with-it cinema recently, to get back to the frank and wholesome vulgarity of the Carry On crowd. This time they are romping around in French Revolution garb in *Don't Lose Your Head*. Where would our film industry be without them? Like Brighton without comic postcards or the piers. Or England without the possibility of a pint and sixpennyworth? The jokes are older and bluer than last century's Gorgonzola. The puns are excruciating. Ninety per cent refer to the usually covered quarters of the human anatomy. Underlined, so you can't miss them, with a waiting space for belly laughs. The colour glistens gorily, the crowd scenes are hectic and atmospheric, the photography is extremely good and the whole cast revel in this earthy, amateurish pantomime with glee. Overgrown infants and connoisseurs of vulgarity: rejoice!

1967

'Youngsters in search of drug addicts' ran the headline of the first Brighton and Hove Herald for 1967. 'A team of young people', ran the story, 'will search the streets around Brighton's Clock Tower tomorrow night for drug addicts, beatniks and teenagers with nothing to do. These Christian crusaders - they call themselves 'The Fishers' - are the reconnaissance troops in a big campaign against addiction, which is being waged by an organisation headed by local clergymen. Their aim is to invite as many youngsters as possible back to a hall at the Union Church for refreshments and a talk. Already they can claim one victory - a young girl drug addict on the run from the police, who gave herself up and started a new life after attending one of their meetings.' The Reverend David Copestake, a twenty-six year-old Methodist minister, one of several on the committee of church people behind the scheme said: 'drug addicts need more than just medical care. They need some sort of spiritual power inside them. This is what we are trying to give them.' The Herald was quick to point out though, in the same article, that the minister had himself been found guilty of illegal drug possession the very same week!

In January 1967, the Council were granted clearance orders on 129 'slum' properties in ten streets between Brighton Station and London Road. These were in Kensington Street, Redcross Street, Pelham Street, St Peter's Street, Belmont Street, Providence Place, London Street, New York Street, Fleet Street and York Hill. 'The area will still have to be inspected independently by Ministry officials and an enquiry held into objections,' reported the Argus, 'but between Whitehall and Brighton's Health department there is a 99.9% record of agreement on cases of this kind.' It was reckoned about 440 people would be affected, all to be rehoused by the Council. 'From part of the rubble,' the Argus continued, 'will spring the extension of the Technical College. A car park is planned. The houses in Kensington Street will disappear to make way for a brand new link road between New England Road and Church Street. Details for the remaining areas are at present vague.' The link road was never built, partly due to four houses in Kensington Street being excluded from the compulsory purchase order, on recommendation of the inspector from the government's Housing and Local Government department, who looked into the matter. So not quite 99.9% agreement for once! However, a number of other properties in Francis Street, Ann Street and Cheapside were added to the initial list and demolition approved. We tend to think clearance of slum housing happened in Brighton during the 1930s, but it continued after World War II, right through the 1950s and well into the 1960s. Even in the Carlton Hill area, which saw huge clearance work in the 1930s, several slum streets survived until the 1960s.

In January 1967, Lily Flynn, the mother of Hollywood star Errol Flynn, who lived in McWilliam Road, Woodingdean, died in the Royal Sussex County Hospital. This was following a road accident near the Downs Hotel, where she was hit by a bubble car.

January also saw a £30,000 scheme (that got through 'by the skin of its teeth') for 642 more parking meters in the town. Councillor Sam Taylor, the Highways Committee chairman, said there would be suffering to residents, but there was no other solution to parking problems. 'We have got to keep the wheels of Brighton turning. The alternative is traffic anarchy.' The areas involved were between Brighton Station and London Road, plus the Montpelier area. Councillor Alfred Feld declared: 'Meters are killing Brighton both as a holiday resort and a shopping centre. The last thing we want is any more of these dreadful, two-headed monsters.'

The second stage of Brighton's new Art College neared completion in January 1967. Built at a cost of £268,000 this was the section at the Carlton Hill/Grand Parade corner - seen opposite above - housing the fine art and graphic design studios, plus a lecture hall, library, refectory and kitchens. The new building would be officially opened in June by the president of the Royal Academy, Walter Monnington.

'Work on the third stage,' the press reported, 'to be built at a cost of approximately £170,000 in Grand Parade, is expected to start after the site has been cleared, probably in October this year. It will house the administrative offices, more graphic design studios, photographic studios, an exhibition room and lithographic, silk-screen and leaf-printing departments.'

In March 1967, Brighton's second oldest school closed. This was the Central Voluntary School in Church Street, seen below, directly opposite the end of New Road. When opened in 1828, being a church school, it was under the jurisdiction of St Nicholas Church, which was then the Parish Church of Brighton (later it would be St Peter's). Most of the land then north of Church Street was open countryside and the Royal Pavilion was still a royal residence. Virtually all the children would transfer to a new school building, St Paul's School, in Centurion Road, built to replace the older school of the same name, behind St Paul's Church in West Street, seen on page 93. Two 'old boys' of note were Dennis Hobden, now MP for Kemp Town, and Sidney Bellman, founder of the well-known chain stores.

With several of the new 1960s developments in place and 'up and running', people could see just what they now had to live with. A scathing attack on some of them came from the town's Regency Society in March 1967. 'In a report published yesterday,' announced the Brighton and Herald on its front page, 'the Regency Society of Brighton and Hove condemned the massive Top Rank Entertainments Centre at the foot of West Street, the 320-foot tower block of flats behind the Hotel Metropole, and Cavendish House, a new block of flats near the West Pier. The Top Rank building - their main target - they

described as 'a blind façade', 'a shocking waste of a site' and 'a severe blow to the quality and character of Brighton'. Their objection to the Metropole scheme (Sussex Heights) was its height, and on Cavendish House, the 'lamentable' use of black brick. In an attack on Brighton Planning Committee they say it is almost impossible to understand how the plans of such a building as the Top Rank centre came to be passed. The Town Clerk told the Herald: 'The three buildings mentioned were all designed by prominent architects of international repute. Advice was also sought and obtained from Sir Hugh Casson, Brighton's planning consultant. In the case of the Top Rank building and Cavendish House he required a number of amendments. In all three buildings Sir Hugh's advice was obtained before the brick and other finishing materials were selected. In the case of the Cavendish, six trial walls or panels of various colours of bricks were erected on the site before a final selection was made.'

'It is not always wise to criticise until the building is completed in its final surroundings. When Sir Hugh chose the dark brick he had in mind the new Bedford Hotel arising on the other corner of Cavendish Place and the two buildings will complement each other. This design, as well as Sussex Heights, has been approved by the Royal Fine Arts Commission.'

Referring to the Top Rank building, the Town Clerk said: 'It is quite impossible to assess this building, yet to be completed. Both Top Rank and the Corporation intended from the start that this important site should be enhanced by the use of illumination on its façade. A Top Rank spokesman yesterday repeated a statement made earlier when the Entertainments Committee was under criticism. 'The exterior design has nothing whatsoever to do with the Rank Organisation,' he said. 'It is a matter between Brighton Corporation and the developer.'

The Regency Society's report also commented: 'Perhaps the most alarming feature of the year has been the outcrop of new buildings not necessarily replacing old buildings of distinction but which are - in use of the mildest term possible - ill-designed and ill-sited.'

Despite this outburst, progress continued on all fronts and Churchill Square was largely completed in 1967, final clearance work coming with the removal of the shops fronting Western Road. The view here shows them intact back in November 1961, the other (next page) as

Dorothy Norman's clothing store on the left. A tiny part of this street still exists today opposite the two pubs at the top of Cranbourne Street.

In May 1967, the murder of twelve-year-old Keith Lyon shocked not just Brighton, but the whole country. He was stabbed to death while crossing fields in the Happy Valley area of Woodingean. His father was the well-known local musician Ken Lyon, and who led The Ken Lyon Trio, often performing in the gardens adjoining the Pavilion and Dome during the summer months. To this day, no one has been charged with what still appears to be an apparently motiveless crime.

Those organising the first Brighton Festival of April 1967 could hardly have foreseen the huge event it would escalate to and it remains one of the most important developments of 1960s Brighton. The first festival ran from 14th - 30th April and had an 'all-seeing eye' as its logo, seen on the flags in the picture here, being set up in Old Steine.

they were about to come down six year later, in April 1967. All the owners were offered alternative accommodation in the new square, but most turned down the offer flat, claiming they had, 'been priced out of the market by the Corporation's over-ambitious plans'. Ernest Ward, the greengrocers, declared: 'We opted out at a very early stage. With rentals as high as £8000 the corporation aren't going to get many traders like us in their new square. All they can hope to attract there are luxury firms wanting a shop window'.

The manager of neighbouring Polyfoto Ltd said, 'We shall be going to larger premises in West Street. I am glad we are not moving into the square. I think it will be a white elephant and will take at least five years to get off the ground'.

Demolition of the shops was scheduled to begin on 19th May. In the 1961 picture, the turning to Upper Russell Street can be seen next to

The opposite view shows a sculpture entitled 'Inter-67' about to be installed in Regency Square. This consisted of red, blue, yellow and black plastic globes arranged to form an 'environmental structure' ten feet tall. Student fashions are also seen on the West Pier, the girl sitting appearing to be a Twiggy look-alike.

'Brighton's Festival of the Arts will open the summer season with a bang,' reported the Brighton and Hove Herald. 'The first night alone, April 14th, will be marked by an international wine festival, a visit from the Warsaw Philharmonic Orchestra and a gay arts ball with thousands dancing till dawn at the Metropole exhibition suite. Outside, there will be music along the Sea Front already resplendent with spring flowers, and the first of several firework displays. For fourteen days this 'festival for everyone' will entertain thousands of visitors and residents alike. Thousands of inquiries are pouring into the Festival headquarters in Royal York Buildings from all over the world. The inquiries come from universities, schools of music and organisations who want block bookings. From abroad most inquiries have come from America, Canada, Germany, France, South Africa and Sweden. In Great Britain they have come from twenty counties as well as Scotland and Wales.'

Theatrically, the hottest ticket of the first Brighton Festival was for 'The Dance Of Death', at the Theatre Royal presented by the National Theatre, starring Sir Laurence Olivier and Geraldine McEwan. Interestingly, way down the cast list for this play were three 'sentries', one being future star Anthony Hopkins.

A stunt of the first festival that famously backfired was an ambitious plan to 'paint' a huge Union Jack on the surface of the sea between the piers. 'I want to stress that this is an experiment,' said Ian Hunter, the festival's director. In the picture on the next page, well-known local fisherman Alan Hayes (standing) is seen out in his launch, *Fair Chance,* with artist William Mitchell and assistants, who are putting the special dye onto the sea. The plan for a Union Jack had to be scrapped, as the dyes needed were unavailable, so the idea was to just change the colour of the sea. 'The only effect', wrote the Argus, was large splodges of fluorescent sickly green, which lasted more than an hour, discolouring the briny.'

Alan Hayes filled in the detail: 'They arrived with a spray gun and two five-gallon drums of very concentrated crystals. Turning into the wind, the boat hit a wave and a cup of crystals flew into the air, covering the crew. Spray hit them and they all turned green.'

'I feel it has been an interesting interlude in the festival events,' William Mitchell said afterwards. He was also working on a sculpture, 'The Spirit Of Brighton', to stand in the Churchill Square development.

The West Pier was used for several events including what the festival programme called 'Kinetic Audio Visual Environments' with pop group Pink Floyd playing at the Kinetic Area Discotheque most nights from 10.30 until 1.30 am, for an admission of 5/- (25p today). The programme explained:

K4, which is featured in two halls on the West Pier, presents a series of environmental experiences. These owe a greater allegiance to the present-day electric world and its scientific concepts than to the traditional media of the arts. The Area provides a performance situation with both live performers and automatic machines. The Labyrinth is a succession of experiences of space, movement, light, sound, reflection and image. It is entirely automatic, although parts are triggered by the spectator.

Sadly, no photographs of these 'environments' seem to exist.

Musically, the big event was the opening concert at the Dome by the Warsaw Philharmonic Orchestra, performing works by two living Polish composers plus Brahms' Fourth Symphony. Other orchestras and musical groups included the Bournemouth Symphony Orchestra, the English Chamber Orchestra, the Brighton Philharmonic, the Vesuvius Ensemble and the Brighton Festival Ensemble. The BBC Symphony Orchestra closed the Festival with works by Mozart, Elgar and Beethoven, with Yehudi Menuhin as soloist.

Pop acts to appear included The Who, The Cream, Crispian St Peters, The Merseys and Georgie Fame and The Blue Flames. Cleo Lane and John Dankworth were the main jazz attraction.

There were a number of examples of what was known as 'concrete poetry' displayed around the town during the festival. It was presumed that this meant poetry that existed in some other form other than on paper.

So words, groups of words or two or three lines of words appeared at random round the town, at best amusing, at worst totally obscure in meaning. There was even a raft, moored a quarter of a mile out at sea, between the piers, which had three pylons on it bearing the words 'LOVE', 'PASSION' and 'BEAUTY' in large letters. Constant movement and spray dislodged them after a while until they seemed about to wilt completely. 'All passion bent', was a remark heard from one onlooker.

The last of the quirkier events was a 'Bonfire of Vanities' on the beach. People were encouraged to come and throw anything they

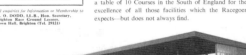

considered ugly into the flames. There were many outrageous suggestions, of course, but few actual offers; the event literally fizzled out.

The first Brighton Festival was judged to be a huge success; it was estimated that it had brought an extra 70,000 extra visitors to the town and run at a loss of only £4000. It was instantly decided to repeat the event the following year and make it an annual event. An extraordinary new era in Brighton's artistic fortunes had begun.

In May 1967, everyone sat up when the Brighton Herald gave news that the Hippodrome was to reopen in the autumn. It was owned by Moss Empires which had negotiated with Mecca Ltd (most well-known for running the Miss World Beauty contests) for a long-term lease on the old theatre. They sat down again when a spokesman said the Hippodrome would be used for 'entertainment and catering', but not what form this would take. Although dancing was mentioned, as it turned out, the 'entertainment' offered would be bingo, much to the dismay of theatre-goers who had hoped they would see twice-nightly variety make a come back.

Also in May, a new £42,000 Baptist Tabernacle was opened in Montpelier Place. This replaced a much older 1834 church that stood behind West Street, demolished for the Churchill Square shopping complex. So many people wanted to attend the opening of the new 250-seater church that the dedication service had to be relayed to every room of the new building and to a marquee on the adjoining car park.

As we did in 1961, let's digress from main events and developments to look at another of the town's publicity guidebooks, this time the one for 1967.

It's remarkably similar to the 1961 brochure and still isn't really promoting conference facilities in any major way; it only devotes a page to the town being a 'conference and exhibition centre' advertising the Top Rank Entertainment Centre, with facilities for 4000 delegates. There's a page, too, on the Brighton Festival, outlining the main events, but asking visitors to 'please send a postcard for details'. However, again, the main emphasis is firmly on family holidays, simple seaside fun and days out to neighbouring towns and villages.

The few concessions to the progress of the decade are the Grand Hotel advertising ease of parking by having 'a multi-storey car park behind the hotel' (the one seen being built on page 80) and it does say it's 'one of the finest conference hotels in the country'. The

250-room Hotel Metropole promotes its Starlit Room rooftop restaurant and casino - 'Britain's first Continental-style Casino' - as its top attractions.

The 'eating out' section of the guidebook has a half-page advert - seen top of the previous page - for the Top Rank Suite, 'the new venue for banqueting and dancing'. The Aquarium is advertising its motor museum; entrance to the Aquarium was 2/- for adults, 1/- for children, but the motor museum cost an extra 2/6d for adults, 1/6d for children.

Sporting amenities are heavily featured again, with Brighton and Hove dubbed 'the sports centre of the south'. 144 bowls links, 4 pitch and putt courses, six golf courses, open air and indoor swimming pools, plus indoor golf and cricket nets, are listed, plus all the attractions of the King Alfred. These included ten-pin bowling, indoor bowls, table tennis, a physical culture club (meaning bodybuilding), amateur boxing club, swimming clubs, crazy golf, plus 'golf-o-tron', where you seemingly played at a famous golf course (there was a choice of four) but in reality was a projected image on a screen (you didn't even have to move, except take your swing). The new stand at Brighton Racecourse is pictured several times (previous page), along with ice skating (the Top Rank rink), yachting, football, greyhound racing and athletics at Withdean Stadium.

Hotel prices again aren't given, but most of the smaller ones, such as the Granville Hotel at 125 King's Road, right on the seafront, were offering bed and breakfast accommodation from 7 guineas a week. This particular hotel had 'conference delegates welcome' included in its advert. Stage and screen star Dora Bryan had a full-page advert for her hotel - 'Bryan's Hotel' at 62 and 64 Marine Parade. Her prices were 'according to season', at 15-17 guineas, full board.

In June, the eighty-three year-old Brighton firm of Edlins sold up to the Watney group. Founded in 1885, Edlins owned eleven pubs and five off-licences in the town at the time of the sale.

Also in June 1967, it was most definitely the end of another era for many, many people, when the Regent Ballroom closed. This dance hall was on top of the Regent Cinema in Queen's Road where, today, Boots, the chemists have their huge store, built in 1979. It had opened in 1923 and many bands that would become household names like Nat Gonella, Ted Heath, Billy Cotton and Joe Loss led the dancing during its heyday. It closed because, 'it does not possess the facilities demanded by the public', according to a Rank spokesman (he didn't elaborate!).

Although the new Top Rank Suite, at the bottom of West Street, was up and running, the Regent's closure was still unexpected, particularly as just four years earlier, Rank had given it a £15,000 face-lift, laying a completely new dance floor (of Canadian Maple wood) and installing new carpets and furniture.

END OF AN ERA

The final night's dancing was to the sound of Denny Holland and his band - the last resident group at the Regent - and people of all ages gyrated to the frug, shake, twist and monkey (dance crazes then) before a final conga saw the night out. The Regent then became a full-time bingo hall (it was already running bingo sessions four nights a week) but eventually Rank closed this too.

A surprising footnote to all this is when a group called Big Apple Promotions revamped the ballroom, opening in November 1970. Acts here would include Donovan, Chicken Shack, Ginger Baker, Pink Floyd, T Rex, East of Eden, Yes, the Groundhogs, Steppenwolf, Eric Burden and War, Santana and Soft Machine. Fleetwood Mac were scheduled to open the club but 'hassles over the contracts' prevented this.

An event that caused eyebrows to rise in June 1967 was news of a 'raid' on the new casino at the Hotel Metropole leading to five summonses; that roulette had been played unlawfully on three occasions, blackjack on two. This naturally caused a lot of interest, but all charges were eventually dismissed.

Summer shows in Brighton during the summer of 1967 were very thin on the ground. On the Palace Pier 'The Tommy Trinder Show' played, with comedian 'Monsewer' Eddie Gray, the Maple Leaf Four and the Lovely Beach Girls. The big film at this time was the latest James Bond adventure, *You Only Live Twice* showing at the Odeon.

'Brighton, THE College town', ran an Argus article in July 1967. 'Work is expected to start next September on Brighton College of Commerce, Catering and General Studies', it said, 'to add further sparkle to the town's galaxy of colleges'. The site for this college, estimated to cost £1 million, was over 750 acres, and would be bounded by Pelham Street, Cheapside and Whitecross Street (very close to the Theobald House tower). This was the extension to the Technical College opposite the Level and would result in a huge expansion of courses it could offer, along with many more student places. 'Apart from the University of Sussex', stated the article, 'Brighton is already the home to the College of Technology (seen above), the College of Education, the College of Art and the Technical College'. This huge expansion in educational provision is often an overlooked aspect of 1960s Brighton, but would prove extremely significant for the growing cultural ambience that was building in the town during the decade.

Black Rock bathing pool is seen on the next page, in July 1967, where a 'Miss Brighton' contest is being judged, another popular annual event that took place throughout the 1960s. Fourteen girls took part and the winner would be twenty-year old Caroline Bull of Denton Drive- number three in the line up - later to marry Brighton Councillor Geoffrey Theobald (son of Stanley). She won the grand sum of £20. Her parents, on holiday in Italy, didn't even know she'd entered the contest. Second was sixteen-year-old Susan Harris, a dancer from Park View Terrace, with Avril Barber, a model from McWilliam Road, Woodingdean, third. The judges were folk-singers Nina and Frederick, plus Alderman George Lucraft.

In July 1967, at the Brighton courts, a mother of three was jailed for nine months for shoplifting.

'Big Move For Allen West's' announced the Brighton and Hove Herald of August 1967. ' One of the biggest employers in Brighton, Allen West and Co., are to close down their factory in Lewes Road and concentrate their business at their factory at Moulsecoomb. Company secretary Mr J Meares told the Herald

yesterday: ' The buildings in Lewes Road will probably be let. One is reluctant to sell land in Brighton - there is so little of it left.' With 3000 men in their employ, talks about possible further redundancies - in February 1966, 111 men were dismissed - were being held with the unions. But Mr Meares said he could make no comment about how staff would be affected by the move.

The move to Moulsecoomb was to 'increase efficiency and to cut out unnecessary commuting between the two factories.'

September saw the new Bedford Hotel officially opened and was also when a start was made on excavating the large car park that still operates under Regency Square (seen here). This was a much-disputed development, the town's Regency Society describing it as a 'disaster' for the square. Costing £523,000 (double what was initially thought, back in 1963 when first costed), the three-storey car park would have space for 525 cars, and would open at Easter 1969.

In October, scaffolding went up on six houses in Grand Parade (opposite) that would be demolished for the final stage of the new Art College building, already two-thirds complete and occupied. It was hoped it would be finished and up and running sometime in 1969.

A new world record for the number of people who could fit into a Mini was set on Brighton beach during October by 'mini-skirted' students as a Rag Week stunt. The number achieved was twenty-eight and 'even though the front seats were removed it was still quite a squeeze and there were more than a few squeaks and squeals, though luckily no-one was seriously hurt.'

During the 1960s, Brighton's annual Rag Week saw all sorts of similar capers undertaken by the town's student fraternity in the cause of fund-raising for charity. Usually someone famous in the town was kidnapped and held to ransom. Prime Minister Harold Wilson's son, Giles, a student at the College of Education, was the target in 1967, but the stunt misfired because 'somebody grassed.' The weather, too, affected some events and a raft race across Hove Lagoon had to be cancelled for lack of sponsors. One really silly event was students dressed in pyjamas and nighties having cooked breakfast on the roundabout opposite the Palace Pier at eight in the morning. The biggest event was the Rag Ball, to be held at the Hotel Metropole. 'Tickets are selling like hot cakes,' reported the local press, 'though after last year's overcrowded dance, when 6000 managed to force their way in, organisers are restricting admission to 3500.' Topping the entertainment bill would be Junior Walker and the All Stars, with support from the Alan Price Set, the Crazy World of Arthur Brown ('Fire...!'), the Bonzo Dog Doo Dah Band and the Brian Auger Trinity. Charities that would benefit from the 1967 Rag events would be the Copper Cliff Home, Brighton Co-ordinating Committee for Old People's Welfare, and the Brighton and Hove Branch of Save The Children's Fund.

In November, the new Law Court building in Edward Street was officially opened by Lord Gardiner, the Lord Chancellor. The architect was Percy Billington, who had also designed the new Art College; the cost was £665,000.

Nationally, the Wimbledon fortnight of 1967 was the first event to be transmitted in colour by the BBC, and by November colour television was available in Brighton for the first time, piped through transmitting equipment situated on Devil's Dyke. It was thought a hundred sets in the town were ready to receive it.

December saw yet another clearance scheme given the go-ahead. This was for properties in the area of Mount Zion Place, off Church Street, where one householder, George Potter (a corporation road sweeper) of 5 Kew Street, staunchly admitted, 'I'm really not surprised - we knew the house would have to come down.'

Christmas films and shows for 1967 included *Thoroughly Modern Millie* at the Regent, Disney's *Jungle Book* at the Odeon, *Far From The Madding Crowd* at the Astoria and *The Great Race* at the Ace, Lewes Road. The Theatre Royal offered the pantomime 'Cinderella', starring Norman Vaughan as Buttons.

1968

Some Key Events:

January	- Five typists from Surbiton, Surrey, start the 'I'm Backing Britain' campaign.
February	- British Standard Time is introduced.
March	- George Brown resigns as British Foreign Secretary.
April	- Enoch Powell's 'rivers of blood' speech. James Earl Ray shoots Dr Martin Luther King.
June	- Assassination of Robert F Kennedy in Los Angles by Sirhan Sirhan.
July	- Alec Rose, aged fifty-nine, receives a hero's welcome at Portsmouth after 354-day round the world trip.
October	- Marriage of Aristotle Onassis and Jacqueline Kennedy. The Mexico Olympic Games are held. Britain wins five gold medals.
November	- Richard Nixon becomes US President.
December	- Crew of Apollo 8 become first humans to see the far side of the moon.

No 1 in the music charts at Christmas was 'Lily The Pink' by The Scaffold.

Social snippet - In 1968, the average weekly wage in Britain was now £23.

Local Film Review: *The Graduate* (shown at the Odeon)

The moral overtones of *The Graduate* are to me, to be deplored. So Mrs Robinson is a semi-disillusioned alcoholic married lady who takes a young fellow to bed for one purpose. So what? But that I think is the only thing I could seriously pick fault with in the film. You either love it or it leaves you cold. I loved it, particularly the deadpan performance of Dustin Hoffman as the gauche wonder-boy graduate seduced in his own bedroom by, 'Oh Mrs Robinson.'

It's marvellous - his comically perplexed, hands-in-pockets-look - as he lets the world just happen to him. He reminds me of the hero in Salinger's 'Catcher In The Rye'; not that I am over in love with this film. It has a big word of mouth reputation to live up to. Naturally, I went expecting too much.

Films for January included the musical *Half A Sixpence* at the Astoria, *Carry On Follow That Camel* at the Odeon and *The Alamo* at the Curzon. The Regent continued showing *Thoroughly Modern Millie* and *Blow Up* was at the Jacey in North Street. The Theatre Royal continued with its 'Cinderella' pantomime.

Bingo was at the Essoldo, the Ritz, the old Regent dance hall, the Hippodrome, the Odeon, Kemp Town and now - from January - at the former Ace cinema in Lewes Road (which at the start of the decade was the Gaiety - the name changed in 1965), which began offering bingo in the light of falling audiences. Would-be patrons were tempted in during the opening week with twenty games on offer for just 2/-, a free game where the prize was 10000 Green Shield Stamps, plus a top overall prize of £5000.

In January the Corporation announced it would have to increase the cost of deck-chair hire for the 1968 season to 9d. Hove immediately announced their charge would stay at 6d!

'Toys are getting more sophisticated and scientific', ran a short article in a January Brighton and Hove Herald. 'At the British Toy Fair, to be held at Brighton from Sunday to Thursday, there is a chance to see the very latest. Action Man, for instance, now talks. Eight different commands to his men can be given from a revolutionary talking unit in the commander's chest! The Action Man, hitherto seen in the Red Devil's parachute kit, are also supplied with off-duty outfits for football or cricket. Toys, in fact, are becoming as realistic as the real thing. Visitors to the fair will see a midget hovercraft that really hovers. Five venues have been utilized to house this impressive fair - the Hotel Metropole's exhibition halls, the display areas of the Grand Hotel and the new Bedford Hotel, the Top Rank Centre and the Corn Exchange'.

Holiday advertisements leapt out from the local papers during January, with the really low-cost 'package' type given the largest space. Majorca by air for £37 announced Swan Wing Holidays (presumably for two weeks). It also offered fifteen days on the Costa Brava for £36. Other firms, such as Lyons, were offering 'Gems of Italy (ten days) for 33 gns (guineas - a guinea was £1/1/-), fifteen days in Moscow for 65 gns, eleven days in Casablanca for 45 guineas and even ten days in Lido di Jesolo for 19 gns. Far away places with strange sounding names were becoming cheaper and easier to reach.

February 1968 saw Radio Brighton come 'on air'; this was Britain's fifth VHF station. A special programme on the history and development of Brighton was broadcast featuring a stellar cast - Laurence Olivier, Flora Robson, Dora Bryan, John Clements and Alan Melville (all 'locals').

In February one of the most infamous incidents of the whole decade took place when red paint (it was to be pig's blood originally) was thrown over an American press attaché, Robert M Beers, who had spoken about 'Vietnam in Depth' at Falmer House, Sussex University. A US flag was also burnt. This caused a huge fuss and student Sean Lineham, who'd thrown the paint, was suspended. This led to a student 'strike' with picket lines and placards, resolved only by the personal intervention of Professor Asa Briggs, Vice-Chancellor of the University, who said the student's suspension would only be temporary. Later there were accusations that plain-clothed policemen were operating at the University, seeing who might cause further trouble.

February also saw an extraordinary report published by a special committee of Brighton's Junior Chamber of Commerce. This was a 'master plan' envisaging how Brighton would be in the year 2000. As you can imagine, it makes fascinating reading, but only a brief summary can be given here. Chaired by Mr A Elliot and based mainly on views of 'young business and professional men' the report envisaged one local authority between Shoreham and Newhaven, with the name Brighton given to the entire area. The population would be 350,000. 'The administrative seat of the Regional Authority', it said, 'should be housed in an imposing building in the centre, close to the Royal Pavilion; thus being within easy reach of commercial interests and at the same time serving as a focal point.'

'As far as the present Brighton and Hove is concerned', the report continued, 'it is considered that all old and uneconomic buildings should be redeveloped, with the exception of the famous squares, crescents and terraces, ranging from Adelaide Crescent to Arundel Terrace, which form part of the heritage of the area. It is anticipated that most of the present building space within the area will have been utilised by the year 2000, but there must be ample provision for parks, gardens and playing fields, as additions and extensions to the present ones. There must be no building encroachment on the Downs which would spoil this natural and magnificent protective boundary.'

Interestingly, among the many stipulations proposed for new buildings, one in particular - 'plastic, or similar materials will be used for window-frames, etc.' was exactly what would happen with UVPC double glazing.

A questionnaire sent out to all members of the chamber saw sixty-eight percent favouring banning all motor vehicles from the town centre, twenty-two percent banning only certain types of vehicle, with ten percent opposed to banning any vehicles. Traffic congestion was seen as a major problem in 2000 (how right they were!) with tunnelling the answer - one (running one way only) from the Aquarium to Preston Street, 'with access provided from the tunnel to hotels, conference halls and vehicle parks'; another, running in the other direction, would be 'behind the hotels'. Brighton Station would become a monorail terminus, with conventional trains using a huge new station complex at Patcham. Hovercraft services would run from the Marina, Newhaven and Shoreham, providing coastal and cross-Channel services.

A new opera house and exhibition hall in the town would be built and the place would become 'an international arts centre' (again, mostly true). There would be artificial ski slopes on the Downs and 'a Sports Centre for every type of sport. Withdean Stadium will be roofed over for use as an indoor sports arena. There will be an 'endless belt machine' for water skiing between the piers. Part of Madeira Drive sundeck will be glass encased. And the marina will become a yachtsman's heaven.'

There were some very whimsical touches in the report, though, such as the hover-rail service being formally opened by King Charles III and even Brighton and Hove Albion playing international matches against teams like Stuttgart!

In March 1968, the final Parliamentary Bill that would allow Brighton Marina to be built - the actual harbour area - was passed. The voting was thirty-eight against, sixty-seven for. However, there was still a huge way to go. A separate Bill was now needed for the road system, giving access to the site, which the government stipulated would have to be in place before work on the actual harbour began.

A meeting at the Dome (seen here) at the end of the year saw the plans outlined and discussed, with the cost of the whole Marina development now estimated at £14 million.

Filming was taking place on the Palace Pier in March for Richard Attenborough's first film as director, *Oh What A Lovely War;* The theatre was used to recreate scenes from a music hall. The West Pier was also extensively used, as was Sheepcote Valley which, dug up, became the wartime trenches. People especially remember the Downs covered with crosses for the film's final shot, where a helicopter tracks further and further back, showing what must have been several thousand of them; this was filmed later, in May.

At Easter 1968, dolphins appeared at the Brighton Aquarium for the first time. Their success would lead to a full-sized show pool being built the following year.

In May, Brighton College of Education - the new teacher training college at Falmer - was officially opened by Earl Mountbatten of Burma.

It was a disaster of May 1968 - in East London - that brought a virtual halt to the craze for building tower blocks in Britain. Three people were killed when a suspected gas explosion caused the collapse of a twenty-two-storey block of flats known as Ronan Point, in Newham. In Brighton, questions were raised about the safety of high-rise flats in Hollingdean when two blocks there - Nettleton Court and Dudeney Lodge- were found to have defects. The brickwork of Hereford Court and Wiltshire House, off Eastern Road, was eroding too and these concerns, along with discontent from residents about the isolation of high-rise living, saw a stop to the Council building high-rise accommodation.

In May 1968, there was a lot of fuss when part of Sussex Street was renamed Morley Street after former councillor, James William Morley. The change came about due to John Street being extended to Sussex Street (so in effect what used to be Nelson Place was renamed and became a continuation of the existing John Street) and the lower part of Sussex Street was then subsequently renamed. Quite why all this was done mystified everyone and still does today.

May 1968 saw the second Brighton Festival take place; '100 events in sixteen days' were promised. Science Fiction was to be a major theme - an unusual choice. Events for this would include a children's concert entitled 'The Time Machine', composed by Herbert Chappell, 'Mass For Tomorrow', a work for narrator, chorus and 'electronic tape' at St Peter's Church, 'Journey Into Space', a new work by David Gray and the Brighton Youth Orchestra, plus a season of twelve science fiction films, including a new film specially commissioned for the Festival. There would also be a forum on the future of film making presided over by Sir Michael Balcon.

Promised Fringe events included 'a unique spectacle of continuous motion by sea, waves and wind provided by 150 feet high inflatable Seatotems moored between the West and Palace Piers.' The sponsors were naturally hoping that the Seatotems would be more successful than last year's sea towers, spelling out Love, Beauty and passion, which came to grief. 'Every precaution is being taken by British Xyonlite Ltd., and Transatlantic Plastics, the sponsors, to ensure that a similar squall does not rob the Festival of its totems.' The 'totems' would be long, welded, coloured tubes inflated with air and fixed with 'ballast and anchor' to float in a cluster. They would be held vertical by hydrogen-filled balloons and illuminated at night. Another plan, for children, was for a huge, inflated 'Aqua-pneumatic trampoline, filled with coloured fluids, built over the paddling pool near the West Pier.

The two pictures here show items from an exhibition of sculpture in the Pavilion grounds.

The programme of pop concerts, jazz and what was then called 'light music', included Sandie Shaw, singer of Britain's winning entry in the Eurovision Song Contest that year - 'Puppet On A String' - at the Dome, Cleo Lane and John Dankworth in concert at the Palace Pier Theatre, plus the BBC Concert Orchestra giving a programme of popular light classical music at the Dome.

The big opening orchestral concert of the festival would have Sir William Walton conducting his own 'Belshazzar's Feast' performed by the Royal Philharmonic Orchestra. Sir William was to receive the honorary degree of Doctor of Letters from Sussex University during the festival fortnight. Yehudi Menuhin would play two violin concertos and the Chilean pianist, Claudio Arrau would also give a recital.

While the Brighton Festival has continued to flourish, old-style bathing beauty contests are a thing of the past in Brighton. However, the Concours d'Elegance Automobile (meaning, 'elegant gathering of cars'), seen here in full swing on Madeira Drive, in June 1968, is still held. In the picture, Miss Carole Hardy poses on a Lotus Elan, winning for Peter King, its owner, the Mermaid Trophy for most attractive ensemble of car and passenger. The Concours d'Elegance began after World War II and takes place at venues like Stanmer Park.

Seen now is a very derelict Russell Street, which used to run up from the seafront, east of the Grand Hotel, towards Western Road. Nothing here now exists and the site is mostly covered by the 1970s Brighton Centre. Run down over many years, final clearance came in May 1969, for the last stage of the Churchill Square/Brighton Centre development; in fact top right, in the distance, the 'Spirit of Brighton', sculpture can be seen in place, a feature of the original square. This was designed by William Mitchell, seen in the boat on page 105. Also, the old Church of the Resurrection can be seen - the low building, on the extreme right of the brewery, described on page 93.

The view is dominated by the old Cannon Brewery founded in 1821. This started in a small way in the Russell Street home of a John Barnett who, before building his brewery, sold his own home brew round the town on a cart. Successive owners built trade up until the brewery owned 50 pubs. Tamplins took over in 1926, but stopped brewing three years later, the building being used as just a bottling plant. Final closure came in 1965, following a compulsory purchase order. With its long history, the brewery existed for 150 years.

Churchill Square is viewed now in April 1968, six months before it was officially opened. Virtually everything seen earlier has gone, although a small part of Artillery Street can still be made out, on the extreme right, just below centre. The crane in the foreground is being used to construct the eighteen-storey Chartwell Court flats, completed in 1971. Described as 'a dream come true' at this time, 31 of the 58 shops had been let, along with the department stores and supermarket. There was parking for 1000 cars.

Beyond the maze of buildings, the dark, curved roof of the old Regent Dance Hall, in Queen's Road, can be made out. In the far distance, near the top of the picture, are the high-rise flats of the old Richmond Street area,

now dominating this part of eastern Brighton. Edward Street, on the right, wouldn't acquire the American Express building for several more years.

The opposite view is of the unusual, spiral-shaped plaque, unveiled when the square was officially inaugurated, in October 1968.

The Churchill Square complex saw Western Road doubled in width and the neighbouring Clock Tower island, still at its Victorian, 'horse and cart' dimensions, was in the news - again - for being a traffic bottleneck and causing huge congestion in the town centre. 'Since the 1930s', said the Argus of April 1969 'decades of councillors have talked and waffled and decided precisely nothing. And the wretched symbol for all this spectacular inaction is the Clock Tower, presiding in lavatorial splendour over traffic and planning chaos.'

It wouldn't be until the 1970s that traffic flow was finally eased by extensive demolition work at the corner of North Street, where a new Boots superstore went up, allowing for road widening on the eastern side of the tower site. Complete restoration of the Clock Tower followed in 2000-2001 (to everyone's surprise, it has to be said).

Students outside the new College of Art in Grand Parade are seen here in June 1968, where disputes over a number of issues resulted in 'walk-outs sit-ins and teach-ins'. Students at the College of Education also joined in, both colleges receiving

support from the Student Council at Sussex University. It was all a bit of a storm in a teacup really, the art students feeling they were 'not being educated to keep up with the present day' and trainee teachers asking for 'student-staff committees to play a real role in the running of the college.' However, as a result of these 'demonstrations', Brighton Council called for a meeting with Sussex University authorities for a 'full and frank exchange of views' on the behaviour of students, particularly after the paint-throwing and flag-burning incidents on the campus earlier in the year.

In July 1968, three Brighton churches were about to be sold - the Dials Congregational Church in Dyke Road (seen opposite), the Union Church in Queen Square and the Presbyterian Church in North Road. The idea was to build a new Free Church building, more suited to modern needs, from the profits of these sales. This in fact happened, the money actually restoring the church in North Road, which became the Brighthelm Centre. At the time, though, it was all seen as yet another worrying symptom of 'old Brighton' being lost.

Bingo sessions began at the Hippodrome in July 1968. Shows and films for early August included *2001 A Space Odyssey* at the Astoria, *Doctor Doolittle* at the Regent (to be followed by the Julie Andrews musical *Star!*), *The Dambusters* was being rerun at the Curzon, with *Massacre for an Orgy* at the Jacey, showing with *Brutes*. The Theatre Royal had Agatha Christie's whodunit 'Black Coffee'

playing, while on the Palace Pier 'The Happy Holiday Show' featured Dick Emery and the Barron Knights.

Despite New England House opening industry in the central Brighton area has now pretty much dwindled away. Even Allen West, off the Lewes Road, which in the 1960s employed something like 3,500 people, has only just about hung on and today has less than a hundred workers. However, a small industrial estate established at Hollingbury from 1948, expanded considerably in the 1960s. The interior seen here, in August 1968, is of Gross Cash Registers Ltd, its factory built in 1960. This firm was at its peak just before decimalisation in 1971, when changes to cash registers throughout the country generated huge business and three premises on the estate were occupied. However, the firm failed shortly afterwards and all the buildings closed. Wade Engineering subsequently occupied the building and it still stands today. By the 1970s the estate employed over 1600 workers, nearly all in engineering or manufacturing jobs, but successive recessions would reduce this considerably over the next two decades.

A great story was reported in August 1968 about someone using marked cards to win nearly £600 at the Metropole casino. An American visitor - Auguste Thommen - saw where the cards were kept for blackjack and at an opportune moment, quietly removed them. He went to the hotel's restaurant and with a pair of nail clippers, calmly snipped tiny pieces off the cards in a way that would enable him to differentiate them later. In subsequent games, he won £595 before staff became suspicious. He was arrested, ended up in court, convicted and the fine he had to pay was...£100! Who said crime doesn't pay?

The photograph opposite, taken in September 1968, shows a new accident and emergency centre for the Royal Sussex County Hospital in Eastern Road taking

shape. It was eight months away from completion at this time. At a cost of £1 million, as well as new A & E facilities it would also house a new maternity unit, occupying five floors, scheduled to open in the summer of 1970.

October saw Dawkins forge, seen here, situated in Marshalls Row, at the entrance to the Open Market, London Road, sold off for £16,150. Arthur Dawkins (on the left) had run the forge until his death in 1967 and was a well-known local character; he was one of the last blacksmiths to operate in Brighton and traders still using horse-drawn carts could often be seen at his small forge, getting horseshoes fitted 'on the spot'.

In November 1968, the famous luxury train, the Brighton Belle, celebrated sixty years of operation.

Starting up in 1908 as the Southern Belle, the change of name came when Southern Railway took over the old London, Brighton and South Coast Railway and electrified the line to Brighton in 1933. The train became the Brighton Belle - there were several of them - the very last word in luxurious travel. In the 1960s, many Brighton celebrities travelled up to London on the Belle, including Laurence Olivier who kicked up a huge fuss when kippers were withdrawn from the breakfast menu; with the help of boxing promoter Jack Solomons and fellow actor John Clements, he got them reinstated. However, the Brighton Belle seen below, would only just see the 1960s out. By the end of the decade the large number of on-board catering staff proved to be uneconomic and the coaches were getting shabby. Despite the train's popularity, it would be withdrawn in April 1972. However, two of the carriages were later used as part of the Orient Express, which began running again in 1982.

In December 1968, Alderman Dorothy Stringer, Mayoress in 1952, and councillor since the early 1930s, was awarded the Honorary Freedom of the Borough of Brighton, by the Corporation. This rare award was given to 'persons of distinction and persons who have, in the opinion of the Corporation rendered eminent service to the Borough.' Dorothy Stringer was very prominent in education matters between the wars - Dorothy Stringer School was named after her, of course.

Films and shows over the 1968 Christmas period included *Chitty Chitty Bang Bang* at the Regent, the ABC was rerunning *Half a Sixpence*, the Astoria had *Gone with the Wind*, the Odeon *A Twist of Sand* and the Academy was showing *The Sound of Music*. *The Wizard of Oz* was at the Jacey. Definite signs of scraping the barrel here! The Christmas pantomime was 'Aladdin' at the Theatre Royal, starring Bernard Breslaw, Clive Dunn and Yana.

1969

Some Key Events:

January	- Richard Nixon becomes president of USA (succeeding Lyndon Johnson). The last public performance by the Beatles is given on top of the Apple Records studio.
March	- First episode of 'Dad's Army' broadcast by the BBC.
April	- General De Gaulle resigns as President of France.
May	- John Lennon and Yoko Ono perform their 'bed-in' in a Quebec hotel and also record 'Give Peace a Chance'.
July	- First US troop withdrawals in Vietnam.
August	- British troops deployed in Northern Ireland. Actress Sharon Tate and others are murdered - the so-called 'Manson Murders'.
October	- Hundreds of thousands demonstrate across US in protest at the Vietnam War (it wouldn't end for another six years).
November	- John Lennon returns his OBE in protest at the government's support of the Vietnam War.

No 1 in the music charts at Christmas was 'Two Little Boys' by Rolf Harris.

Social Snippet - During the decade of the 1960s, car ownership in Britain doubled, as did the number of people going sailing on a regular basis. Football attendances dropped though, from thirty-three to twenty-five million.

Local Film Review: *The Thomas Crown Affair* (shown at the Odeon)

The Great Train Robbers would kick themselves if they could see this one. Money, money, money, they say, but when you have everything already, like Mr McQueen, the fancy turns to thoughts of kicks of a supposedly unobtainable nature. He devises a bank raid of dastardly cleverness; Hollywood, however, that Mecca of sexual fulfilment, must ripple the pool. Implausibly she is, in this case, the lovely Faye Dunaway, who plays an insurance investigator. The camera works with some split-screen gimmickry which really makes a big impression, but in one straight scene, producer and director Norman Jewison creates the sexiest chess game that ever was.

In January 1969, workmen were involved in opening up one of the arches of the railway viaduct spanning Lewes Road, seen in the background of the picture here. The road had been widened either side of the viaduct leading to a severe bottleneck around the original central arch. Once the structural work at the bridge was finished (scheduled at this time for May the same year), a new section of road would be laid completing a three-mile stretch of continuous dual carriageway from Bear Road to the Brighton boundary at Falmer.

In January, despite the recent government bill, the Corporation announced it would hold a town poll on whether the Brighton Marina should be built. The cost was now estimated at £14 million, but it was emphasised that it would be entirely privately built, with nothing coming out of the rates. The Marina was the mostly hotly debated development of the late 1960s, with page after page in the local papers giving news of progress or lack of progress getting the project up and running, particularly when delays in Parliament had held things up. The phrase that comes to mind is 'two steps forward, one step back', and occasionally, 'two steps forward, two steps back'. It was, still, essentially the new road system needed to access the site that caused most of the stumbling blocks once the main idea had been accepted. Many groups lodged formal objections, including the Quakers, who had a small burial ground alongside the gasometers at Black Rock, which would have to be cleared.

As with Churchill Square, the construction firm was Taylor Woodrow. Mayor Peter Best would inaugurate the lock gates between inner and outer harbours of the Marina in May 1977 and the public were admitted from July 1978. H.M. Queen Elizabeth II would finally, formally, open the Marina in May 1979, by which time the cost had risen to a massive £41 million, and the final version bore no resemblance at all to the proposal seen earlier. Several owners have subsequently revamped the Marina adding housing, pubs, shops plus many other sporting and leisure facilities. The Marina has continued being a hotbed of contention over the years, with recent plans for a massive skyscraper development on one site and a futuristic monorail service connecting it with central Brighton.

The Brighton Film Theatre, in North Street, opened in February 1969, taking over premises that were formerly the Jacey Film Theatre. There were 432 seats. Richard Attenborough introduced clips from *Oh! What A Lovely War,* which he'd shot mostly on location in Brighton the previous year. In fact, during its early months, this cinema saw many personal appearances from movie personalities. Flora Robson, Kenneth More, Edith Evans, Peter Cushing, John Clements and Jack Warner all introduced films in which they appeared. Also in North Street, the Prudential building was virtually finished in early 1969, providing 60,000 sq ft of office space.

Over the years, the 1920s Prince's Hall at Brighton Aquarium had mainly served as a dance hall. Back in 1961 it became a museum for vintage motor vehicles, but the popularity of two dolphins displayed at the Aquarium in 1968 led to the museum being completely transformed into a large pool for full dolphin shows to take place. This is seen under construction in March 1969. The pool was 80' by 30', cost £50,000 to build, held 200,000 gallons of filtered water, with the spectator area seating 1000 people. It opened at Easter that year with two further dolphins from America added to the two already at the Aquarium. Over the years, thousands of dolphin shows were given, becoming a major tourist attraction for the town. In time, though, animal welfare groups, campaigning against dolphin shows, pressurised Brighton Council into closing the pool and the last performances were in December 1990. There were only two dolphins at the pool by then, Missie and Silver, who were taken to the Caribbean, for rehabilitation, in March the following year. The whole Aquarium was subsequently remodelled as a SeaLife centre, at a cost of £1 million, opening at Easter 1991, with the terraces above being largely rebuilt and modernised in 1999-2000.

March saw the loss of All Souls' Church, Eastern Road. There was a spate of church closures in the news at this time, with several Church of England properties being pulled down, as part of 'a diocesan rationalisation scheme' - in other words, too many churches for too few parishioners. Just as today, there was huge concern over the loss of church buildings - history does have a way of repeating itself! St Matthew's Church, in Sutherland Road, had already come down in 1967. The chapel of St Mary and St Mary Magdalene, in Bread Street, had been lost in 1963, the Catholic Apostolic Church, in Carlton Hill, seen here, came down in 1964 for the Art College building and the Salvation Army Citadel in Edward Street was cleared in 1965. The huge Dials Congregational Church was sold off for redevelopment in 1969 and demolished in 1972. Even St Peter's Church seemed threatened at this time, when the Vicar of Brighton, Canon John Keeling, told the Argus (in September 1967) that the church would soon fall down unless funds were raised for its preservation.

In late April, films and shows included *Where Eagles Dare* at the Astoria, *Funny Girl* at the Academy, and *Oliver!* at the Regent. *Baby Love* was at the Odeon, while the Continentale had *Sin, Sun and Sex*. The Theatre Royal had the play 'The Passionate Husband' with George Cole.

In May 1969, the Corporation announced it would spend £10 million rebuilding the entire Whitehawk estate, which mostly went up in the 1930s and was now seen as substandard. This would in fact take place, but not until the mid-1970s.

The third Brighton Festival took place in May - still with the 'all-seeing eye' as its logo - with roaring twenties and the jazz age as one of its main themes. The budget was £4000. It was also decided to represent the arts from one specific country - Czechoslovakia - so events featured a season of Czech films at the new Brighton Film Theatre, the Black Stage Revue on the West Pier (puppet acts performed under ultraviolet lighting) and performances by the Czech Philharmonic Society. On the jazz theme, a materclass would be led by saxophonist Johnny Dankworth and Palm Court tea dances would be held on the West Pier. A whole range of fringe and pop events would take place, as in previous years. Famous names to appear in the festival would include Yehudi Menuhin, Jacqueline du Pre and Artur Rubinstein.

In May (after the festival) the Beach Boys appeared at the Dome, supported by Paul Revere and the Raiders. Also in May, six Sussex University students were fined a total of £445 on LSD drug charges. One called what he had taken, 'a Strawberry Field.'

By June summer shows had started up again including 'The Big Star Show of 1969' at the Dome, starring Harry H Corbett (one half of the famous *Steptoe and Son*), Susan Maughan, Peter Gordeno, drag artist Ricky Renee, Margo Henderson and Monsewer Eddie Gray. On the Palace Pier, Ronnie Corbett seen below, appeared in 'The Corbett Follies'. 'Fast moving,' said a review in The Stage, 'exquisitely dressed and loaded with talent...must be one of the finest shows produced.' Maggie Fitzgibbon was appearing at the Theatre Royal in Bernard Shaw's 'Candida' at this time, but was followed by a rare summer show at the Royal starring Mike and Bernie Winters, Audrey Jeans and Michael Bentine. Films were *Where Eagles Dare* continuing its run at the Astoria, *The Boston Strangler* at the Odeon; the Regent was still showing *Oliver!* and *The Prime of Miss Jean Brodie* was at the Academy.

In August a competition in the Brighton and Hove Herald had a first prize of 1000 Green Shield stamps.

August also saw the strange sight of the traffic roundabout opposite the Palace Pier being used as a camping site, although not for long. Two 'enraged' tourists, Charles Newell and Ruth Oxenbury, who'd been turned away from the Sheepcote Valley camp site at Whitehawk, decided to pitch their tent on the only available site they could find! The photograph in the next page shows them calmly brewing tea!

Opposite, sixties fashions on the West Pier! It's September 1969 and models show off the latest fashions for men. Left, is what was known as a 'highwayman's raincoat', centre is a 'suit' in Crimplene (the actual colour was blue/green), and right is a Kaftan unisex gown. The Bedford Hotel, in the background (right), is the one opened in September 1967, replacing the original 1829 building, demolished after the fire in 1964. The much-derided Cavendish House can also be seen.

The West Pier itself was about to be closed at this time. The seaward end was barred as unsafe in October 1970, then the whole pier was shut down in September 1975. This was all basically due to lack of maintenance and investment following the war, particularly after being bought by the London firm AVP Industries in 1965. An excruciatingly protracted campaign to save the West Pier then began, but ultimately - like the pier itself - this collapsed when funding from the National Lottery, awarded in 1998, was withdrawn. Recent arson attacks have sealed its fate and another major collapse of the remaining skeletal structure can't be far off.

In October 1969, work started on the building that would occupy the old Albemarle Hotel site, in Marine Parade, which had stood empty since 1960. A pub, with six floors of flats would be built, with an underground parking area with room for twenty-one cars.

'Now A Second Churchill Square?' announced the Argus of December 1969. 'Four acres in a near-derelict part of central Brighton may be privately developed on the lines of Churchill Square,' it reported. 'Brighton Corporation Estates Committee are putting the idea to the town council for the area bounded by Church street, Marlborough Place, North Road and Jubilee Street. Eighty percent of the area is already corporation owned and includes the North Road baths. If the plan goes ahead, a new public library would probably be included in the development. One tentative inquiry about the area had already been received for the four-acre site'. No huge shopping centre came about, of course, but the library eventually did - only forty years later!

The Christmas films and shows that ended 1969 - and the decade - were *Ice Station Zebra* at the Astoria, *The Battle of Britain* at the Regent and *Captain Nemo and the Underwater City* at the ABC. The Classic in Western Road had two *St Trinians* films showing. The Theatre Royal was staging 'Play On Love'.

The bells on New Year's Eve rang out exactly as they had done when 1959 became 1960. As the sixties slipped into the seventies, there was partying at various venues across the town including the Old Ship Hotel (dancing here was to Jack Hazeldine's Band - tickets were £3/3/-) and at the Royal Pavilion where a charity ball was staged, in aid of 'Action for the Crippled Child'. In many ways it must have all seemed identical to the New Year's Eve at the start of the decade, just a few years previously. People surely commented on how quickly the ten years of the sixties had passed.

The celebrations were the same, but Brighton itself was unrecognisable.

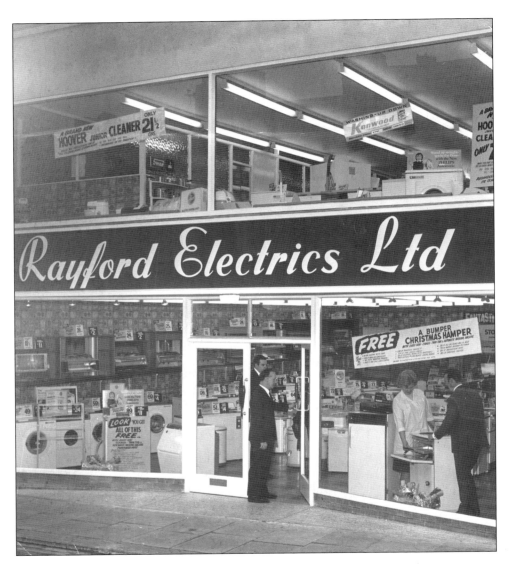

Conclusion

The 1960s was an optimistic decade in British history where technology was seen to be the all-encompassing saviour - the way forward to a better future of increased affluence both for the country and its inhabitants. Rayford's electrical store in Sydney Street is seen here with its newly enlarged showrooms - a true sign of technological times. Harold Wilson, at the Labour party conference of 1960 said: 'This is our message for the Sixties. A Socialist-inspired scientific and technological revolution releasing energy on an enormous scale.' Restrictive laws were abolished or modified (divorce, abortion, homosexuality), ideas of what was acceptable in many areas, particularly music, art and literature changed and the young found both their feet and their voices. Everyone wanted the new gadgets and appliances that were coming out, even the old, as they helped shake off memories of post-war austerity and the rationing imposed then that was even worse than at the height of World War II (rationing ended, finally, as late as 1954); something like a simple hairdryer was considered sheer luxury by those who had never had one.

Brighton saw all this national confidence reflected in its many projects and events, particularly in its new buildings, shopping areas, plus the Brighton Festival, the University and plans for the Marina.

The 1970s would truly bring gloom and doom; the horrific Maria Colwell murder of 1973 would shock the whole nation rigid and lead to a change in the law (the 1975 Children Act) and social service reforms. The Regent cinema would close in 1973. Brighton's last summer shows were held at the Palace Pier Theatre (1973) and the Dome (1974); then variety really was well and truly dead in the town. The drab, grey Brighton Centre would open in 1977, finally completing the rectangle of hotchpotch redevelopment between Western Road, West Street, King's Road and Cannon Place.

Harold Poster died in January 1979. The Argus dubbed him 'the second Dr Brighton.'

And although the Marina would be built at last and opened by the Queen, in May 1979, it began life looking nothing like the 1960s model seen earlier in this book without a single building in it and non-sailing people thinking - initially - there was nothing there for them.

For many the 1960s marked the end of the innocent seaside image the town had cultivated for over a hundred years, since the coming of the railway to the town in the early 1840s; the decade was certainly a watershed. Yet it could be said with some credence that, although decimated by graph paper buildings and redevelopment that is now seen as sterile and mediocre, Brighton emerged with an escalating cultural ambience of real substance - brought about by both its arts festival and new educational

impetus - which probably played a key role in achieving city status in 1999.

Whatever we think of the changes, the buildings, the losses and gains of 1960s Brighton, the place hasn't seen anywhere near the same amount of change actually materialise again, despite several extensive redevelopment schemes (and some currently in the pipeline, including the one between the station and London Road and the King Alfred centre). It all was quite breathtakingly audacious really, and where all the money and drive suddenly came from to achieve so much in so few years is still something to dwell on.

ABOUT THE AUTHOR

Chris Horlock was born in White Street, Brighton, in September 1953 and attended Park Street Infants School (demolished in 1986), St Luke's Terrace Junior School (still there) and the Secondary Technical School, Hanover Terrace (demolished in 2000), where he ran the school tuck shop, organised end of term film shows and drew cartoons of the teachers which were displayed in the school office. He undertook four years of teacher training at what was then Brighton College of Education, Falmer, and his first teaching post was at Glebe Middle School, Southwick, from 1976. He is at present co-ordinator of history and geography at Thomas A Becket Middle School, Worthing, the second largest middle school in the country. He's been married seventeen years to Roz and has two children, Charlotte and George, aged fourteen and ten respectively.

Chris's five other books on Brighton have been immensely successful and he's received correspondence from all over the world from people who have somehow obtained copies of them. His 'Neat And Nippy Guide To Brighton's History' has become a best-selling tourist guide and has spawned a series of similar titles for other towns in Sussex. His next book will be 'Bizarre Brighton', a book detailing all the weird and wonderful stories, facts and figures about the city Chris has discovered or been told over the years. He also writes regular monthly columns in 'Sussex Life' magazine and whizzes all over Sussex giving talks on aspects of Brighton and Hove's history.